30 D

You can read more about Emily and her books at:

facebook.com/profile.php?id =100005373166724&fref=ts
or
twitter.com/EmilyOwenAuthor

30 Days with John

A devotional journey
with the disciple

Emily Owen

Authentic

First published in 2014 by Authentic Media Limited
52 Presley Way, Crownhill, Milton Keynes, MK8 0ES.
authenticmedia.co.uk

British Library Cataloguing in Publication Data
A catalogue record for this book is available from the British Library
ISBN: 978-1-86024-936-5   978-1-78078-0-257-7 (e-book)

Cover design by David McNeill revocreative.co.uk
Printed and bound by Bell and Bain Ltd, Glasgow

for my sisters

Proverbs 17:17a

Acknowledgements

Thank you to my family and friends, I am so blessed to know you.

Thanks to Sheila, my editor. You are an absolute joy to work with. I appreciate your advice, gentle encouragement, affirmation, biblical knowledge and your relationship with God. I am rather fond of your nit-picking eye, too!

As ever, thank you to my heavenly father – to him be all the glory.

Introduction

Your thirty-day journey with the apostle John starts here . . .

John was a fisherman by trade.
He worked in the family business with his father, Zebedee and his brother, James. He left everything to follow Jesus.

John became one of the disciples closest to Jesus, spending time with him and learning from him.
John's life with Jesus was full of ups and downs.
Confusion, hope, despair, joy, privilege.

While the biblical books of 1, 2 and 3 John and Revelation are generally attributed to the apostle John, there is some debate about whether he is actually the author.
This book, however, assumes that he is. (Of course, he also wrote the gospel named after him.)

Each day's reading ends with John's Jottings. This is a challenge, stemming from either the diary entry or its application, to keep in mind throughout the day and to action when appropriate.

Introduction

A 'My response' section follows for you to record anything that may have arisen for you as a result of the day's reading.

John wrote for everyone.
He wrote so that everyone might know Jesus' story.
He wrote so that everyone might know that Jesus is God.
And 'everyone' includes you.

John 3:16 (NLT incl. footnote):
'For God loved the world so much that he gave his one and only Son, so that everyone who believes in him will not perish but have eternal life.'

I pray that John's diary will lead you into a deeper relationship with the God who loves you and has given everything for you.

Emily

[Jesus said,] 'I came that [you] may have life, and have it abundantly.'

John 10:10 (NASB)

Day 1

Well, who would have thought that I would actually keep a diary? Not sure how it will work out as I've never kept one before. How do I start? Writing has never really been my thing – I am too impatient. If things affect me, I'd much rather have a good discussion (OK, usually argument!) about them than write them down. But stuff has been happening that my gut is telling me I should keep a record of.

It all started with John the Baptist. He has loads of people following him, listening to him, learning from him, being baptized by him. They seem to think that he may be the promised Messiah – but John keeps telling them that he's not and that someone even better than him is coming. Better than John?! I'm not sure about that, but there is definitely something going on. I'll keep my eyes and ears open.

Wow, what an opportunity for John the Baptist!
Be the long-awaited Messiah!
John is already popular, but this could take things to a whole new level.

Except, it couldn't.
Because John was not the Messiah.

John was John.
He knew what his calling was.
And he knew what his calling was not.
So, despite other people trying to change that calling,
John stayed true to what he was meant to do.
He did not let other people sway him.
Did not let them persuade him to try to be something
God did not intend him to be.
Do you?

So, here we have a case of mistaken identity.
John, a man called by God to pave the way for Jesus, the
promised Messiah, is actually being thought to be Jesus
himself!
Is being thought to be someone else.

Let's think about identity.
Or, specifically, your identity.
Who you are in God.

Romans 6:18:
'You have been set free from sin.'

Set free from sin.
Set free from being trapped.
Set free from guilt.
Set free from beating yourself up about things.
Set free from bad choices you've made.
Set free from your past.
Set free from . . .

That's your identity!
Or at least, it can be.
Is it how you identify yourself?
How others identify you?
As set free?

Or do you, and they, see someone else?
Someone who is trapped, guilty, burdened, not worth
very much?
Someone not living their true identity in God?
Someone not living as the person God called them to
be?
Someone who is living a life of mistaken identity . . .

Clothes are often the first thing we notice about other
people.
What we wear can communicate a message about who
we are.
For example, a policeman on duty, in uniform, does not
need to announce that he is a policeman.
But if he was off-duty, wearing casual clothes, he would
quite possibly not be taken for a policeman.

Colossians 3:12:

*'Therefore, as God's chosen people, holy and
dearly loved, clothe yourselves with compassion,
kindness, humility, gentleness and patience.'*

This verse tells us what our spiritual uniform is.
The clothes God has specially picked out for us to wear.

For you to wear.
Compassion. Kindness. Humility. Gentleness. Patience.
The clothes you are to put on . . . and not take off.
Because God's chosen people are never off-duty.

But sometimes we forget.
We forget to dress as God's chosen people.
We forget to be compassionate.
We forget our identity in God.
We forget who God called us to be.
And so we become people who live a life of mistaken identity.

2 Corinthians 5:17:

'If anyone is in Christ, he is a new creation; the old has gone, the new has come!'

The old has gone!
You've been set free from who you used to be.
Your identity does not need to be wrapped up in who you were!

God is a God who moves on.
A God who makes things new.

Your identity is in Christ – don't let yourself forget it.
Don't let yourself slip back.
Don't let yourself live a life of mistaken identity.

Day 1

Lord God,

Thank you that you chose me.
That you called me.
That you gave me an identity in you.
I'm sorry for the times when I try to live a life of mistaken identity.
Help me to hold on to your promises – and help me to believe them.
Really believe that the old has gone . . .

Amen

John's Jottings

My identity is
in God

My response:

Day 2

Well, it seems John the Baptist was right . . .
something happened today and I am so glad I didn't
miss it. A man I know called Jesus showed up and it
turns out that he's the Messiah. So, it's not John after
all.

It happened while John was baptizing people in the
River Jordan, as he often does. I wasn't really paying
much attention until I became aware that John had
stopped baptizing and was just standing in the river.
And he wasn't alone – Jesus was standing in the river
with him. I looked over and saw that they were having
some sort of discussion, so I went closer to try to find
out what was going on. They were talking about Jesus
getting baptized. Jesus wanted John to do it, but John
was reluctant. I thought that was strange; John loves
baptizing people. But he was trying to put Jesus off,
saying that Jesus should baptize John, not the other
way round. This went on for a while until, in the end,
John agreed and Jesus was baptized. It was amazing
– as Jesus came up out of the water, there was a voice
from heaven: 'This is my Son, whom I love; with him
I am well pleased.'

Let's take a look in more detail at what the voice from heaven – God's voice – said as Jesus was baptized (Matthew 3:17).

This is my Son
God is laying his cards on the table here.
He wants everyone to know who Jesus is.
Who Jesus belongs to.
There is a sense of pride in these words.
God did not have to say them; he chose to.
And he did not whisper them, either.
He didn't try to hide them.
God looked at Jesus and said, 'This is my Son'.
Everyone, take note – this is *my* Son.

What does God say when he looks at you?
Does he say, 'This is my son/daughter'?
You can be sure that he wants to . . .

John 1:12 (NLT):
'But to all who [believe] him and [accept] him, he [gives] the right to become children of God.'

All who believe and accept him.
Not some.
Or those who are good enough.
Or those who never have problems or worries.
All.
Everyone can be a child of God.
Everyone.

You can have God look at you and say, 'This is my son/daughter.'
And, when God looks at you and says those words, he won't be whispering.

Whom I love

'This is my Son *whom I love.*'

Just as God said it to Jesus (Mark 1:11), so he says it to you –
'You are my son/daughter *whom I love.*'
Maybe you know that.
Maybe you have known for a long time that God loves you.
Maybe it is old news.
And, maybe, over time it has become head knowledge?
Something you know but forget to enjoy?
Forget to live in the reality of?

When was the last time that you simply enjoyed the fact that God loves you?
That he thinks you are worth something?
That, even though he knows you inside out, he loves you.
Whatever happens, God never forgets that he loves you.
Never forget to remember it . . . and enjoy it!

Love is often expressed through close relationship.
Through having a particular affection for someone.

That's what God and Jesus enjoyed.
A special relationship.
Jesus was the object of God's special affection.
Let's just take a look at that in a bit more detail . . .

They had been together from the beginning.
In heaven.
And then Jesus left heaven and came to earth.
God sent him.
Jesus left the splendour of heaven and came and lived on earth.
Was born in a stable, was poor, was ridiculed . . . and yet he was the object of God's special affection.

What?
Does God just have a funny way of showing it?!
Or is there maybe something else going on here?
Well, yes there is, and that something can be summed up in the word 'relationship'.
Throughout everything that was going on, God and Jesus maintained their special relationship.
They talked with each other.
The Bible tells us of many times when Jesus went off to talk with God (see Luke 5:16).

When God says 'I love you', he means that you are the object of his special affection. He means that he wants to maintain a special relationship with you.
And that means you need to talk together.
Whatever is going on in your life, good or bad, talk to God.

Maintain that relationship with him.
And know that, in the midst of the whirlwind of life,
you are the object of God's special affection.

With him I am well pleased

God is not just pleased with Jesus here, he is well pleased.
God looks at Jesus, his Son, whom he loves, and he is
well pleased.
Jesus gives God pleasure.
What about you?
Do you give God pleasure?
By what you do? What you say? How you live?
Jesus knew what God wanted him to do, what kind of
life God wanted him to live – and he did it.
His baptism marked the start of his ministry.
And that is what gave God pleasure.

Do you know what God wants you to do?
And, more importantly, whether it is something big or
something small, do you do it?

Sometimes it can be hard to know exactly what God is
asking of us . . .

Romans 12:2 (emphasis mine):

*'Do not conform any longer to the pattern of
this world, but be transformed by the renewing
of your mind.* Then *you will be able to test and
approve what God's will is – his good, pleasing
and perfect will.'*

The more you set your mind and heart on God and not the world, the more you will be changed into someone who is able to find out what God is asking of you.
Find out how God wants you to live.
And you will give God pleasure.
God will be able to say of you, not only that you are his child, not only that he loves you to bits . . . but that with you, he is well pleased.

Lord God,

I am your child and you love me.
Thank you that I can say those words
and know that they are true.
I love you, too, Lord.
I want to give you pleasure, every minute of
every day.
Whatever comes my way, help me to handle it
in a way that pleases you.

Amen

John's Jottings

Give God
pleasure

My response:

Day 3

More and more people are following Jesus. In fact, he is actually asking them to follow him. Some are even stopping following John and turning to Jesus instead. And, get this, Jesus is not only asking people to follow him – he has now picked twelve he wants to follow him extra closely . . . and I'm one of them!

I am really pleased, I would like to follow Jesus. I know I am only just starting out with him, but I can already tell that he's pretty amazing.

It happened just after a long fishing trip. We had done OK, got quite a good catch. Afterwards, of course, we had to repair the nets. I am not too keen on this bit, but it has to be done. So there I was, with my brother James, fixing our nets, when along came Jesus. He called us straight away, both James and me, and we left everything behind and followed him. Maybe that seems a bit crazy, but we did not give it a second thought, we just knew it was the right thing to do.

So now, I am not only 'John the fisherman', I am 'John the disciple of Jesus', too.

So, crowds have been following Jesus.
It was probably exciting for them.

Jesus was something new, everyone was talking about him and no one wanted to miss out on the latest trend. Which was great.
But Jesus wanted more than that.

He wanted people who would do more than just follow him without commitment.
He wanted people who would go through ups and downs with him, share with him, learn from him – people who would spend their lives with him.
So he chose twelve men.
Twelve very different men.
Fishermen, tax collectors, right-wing, left-wing, educated, uneducated, peaceful, hot-tempered . . . pretty much as diverse a group as possible.

And yet, Jesus brought them together. Deliberately.
Knowing that they wouldn't always see eye to eye with each other.
Knowing that they would argue.
Knowing that they would get competitive and jealous.
Knowing that they would sometimes get it wrong.

Now, why would Jesus do that?
Why not choose a group of like-minded people?
Surely that would be easier?

Let's fast-forward two thousand years . . .
Jesus wants people who will do more than just follow him without commitment.

He wants people who will go through ups and downs with him, share with him, learn from him – people who will spend their lives with him.
So he chooses . . . the church.
Different.
Diverse.
And yet Jesus brings us together.
Deliberately.
Knowing that people in the church won't always see eye to eye with each other.
Knowing that we will argue.
Knowing that we will get competitive and jealous.
Knowing that we will sometimes get it wrong.

But knowing that we are all essential to the completeness of the whole.

As Paul wrote to the church in Corinth (1 Corinthians 12:27):
'You are the body of Christ, and each one of you is a part of it.'

Each individual is part of the whole and, without each one, something is missing.
You are vital.
You have a place in God's church – are you filling it?

1 Corinthians 3:9:
'You are . . . God's building.'

Ephesians 2:21,22:
'In him [Christ] the whole building is joined together and rises to become a holy temple in the Lord. And in him you too are being built together to become a dwelling in which God lives by his Spirit.'

You are chosen.
But maybe you think Jesus would have been better to choose someone cleverer,
or smarter,
or more talented than you.
Surely that would've been easier?

Jesus didn't want easier.
He wanted the best.
Which is why, when he looked at the world – at the place where you live, work, spend time, at the situations you come across – he saw a gap.
A gap to serve him.
A gap that only you could fill.
Are you filling it?

After Jesus called John, 'John, the fisherman' also became 'John, the disciple'.

Whatever your background, whatever your job, whoever you are, can you also say,
'I am a disciple, I am a committed follower of Jesus'?

Lord God,

Thank you that you are sovereign.
You see the bigger picture and, in that picture, you see the gaps.
Which you send people to fill.
Help me to fill the gaps where you have placed me, by bringing you into every situation I come across.
Lord, help me to follow you with commitment as I live my life, and so truly be able to call myself your disciple.

Amen

John's Jottings

I'm a
disciple

My response:

Day 4

Unbelievable! I can hardly believe what happened today – I'd better write it down or I'll begin to think I dreamed it!

We were in Jerusalem for the Passover feast and were just walking past the pool of Bethesda. As always, there were lots of disabled people lying near the pool. People believe that, when the waters move, the first person into the pool will be healed. I've walked that way before but never stopped, and I probably wouldn't have stopped this time if I hadn't heard Jesus talking to someone. I turned to look and saw that he was talking to a man who was paralysed. Jesus had seen the man and subsequently found out that he'd been paralysed for thirty-eight years. So Jesus asked the man if he wanted to get well. I mean, what sort of question is that?! Of course the man wanted to get well . . . or so I thought, anyway. But his answer surprised me. There was no, 'Yes, please!' Instead he said that he couldn't – because he had no one to help him to the pool and so would never be able to get there first. In response, Jesus looked at him and said, 'Get up! Pick up your mat and walk.' And, you know what? The man did.

How good are you at noticing?

Life is so busy these days that it can be easy not to notice when other people are struggling.

The story in today's entry happened when there would have been lots of people in Jerusalem. They were there to celebrate the feast of Passover. To remember the amazing way in which God had helped their ancestors escape slavery in Egypt (Exodus 12 – 14).

It would have been noisy.

It would have been busy.

People would have been pushing and shoving as they tried to make their way around.

Tried to get to where they wanted to go.

Too busy to focus on anyone but themselves.

Except for Jesus, that is. He noticed.

Actually, he more than noticed.

He stopped.

He didn't rush by, focused on his own agenda.

He recognized that nothing is more important than people – and so he stopped.

How good are you at stopping?

Do you make time for people?

Remember the verse from Colossians?

'Therefore, as God's chosen people, holy and dearly loved, clothe yourselves with compassion, kindness, humility, gentleness and patience.'

So, Jesus saw, then stopped, then spoke.
But, before he spoke, he took to time to find out about the man.
He was interested.
He listened.
He took time to understand where the man was coming from.
That he was coming from a disabling situation he had been living with for thirty-eight years.
Jesus saw the man as a person, not a problem to be immediately dealt with and fixed.

Do you see people or problems?
Do you bother to try to understand where people are coming from?
Why they do what they do?
Why they say what they say?

Then Jesus asks the man a question (John 5:6):
'Do you want to get well?'
Or, in other words, 'Do you want me to sort it?'
And we wait for the, 'Yes, please' that doesn't come.
The man focuses on the obstacles.
On the difficulties.
On the reasons why he can't get well.

He overlooks the one who is asking the question.
He overlooks Jesus in his haste to list the obstacles.

Does that ring any bells with you?

Do you overlook Jesus in your haste to count the obstacles?

Matthew 11:28:

[Jesus said,]
Come to me, all you who are weary and burdened,
and I will give you rest.'

Come to me . . .
What's your response when Jesus says to you, in your situation,
'Do you want me to sort it?'

Is it, 'But . . . But . . . But . . . what about x/y/z?'
Or is it, 'Yes, please', as you hand stuff over to him?
It's your choice.
He's there.
He's waiting.
But it is up to you to let go.

Lord God,

Sometimes I am bad at noticing.
And even worse at stopping.
Please help me to get my priorities right.
To remember that nothing is more important than people.
And help me to remember that 'people' includes me.
I'm important, too.
I do want you to sort stuff, but sometimes it is hard to let go of my problems – help me to have the courage to say 'yes, please' and hand things over to you.
Thank you that I don't have to do it on my own.

Amen

John's Jottings

Hand over
to God

My response:

Day 5

It's been a bit of time since I wrote in this diary. Told you writing wasn't really my thing. Life has been good, following Jesus around, watching and learning from him. Some people don't seem to like him much, but most do. Which probably explains what happened today.

We (Jesus and his disciples) were sitting on a mountainside, chatting. Just us. Then Jesus looked up and saw a crowd coming, on their way to find him. I think it's because the people must have heard about the miraculous things Jesus has been doing. Anyway, they were all climbing the mountain and Jesus asked Philip where was the best place to buy bread to feed them. I felt really sorry for Philip. I mean, I know he comes from the area, so might have a vague idea, but there were over five thousand people in that crowd! As Philip pointed out, eight months wages wouldn't even feed them all. But then Andrew saw a boy who had brought a picnic. Five loaves and two fish. Jesus took them from him and made those loaves and fish feed the whole crowd – there were even twelve baskets left over! I know, because I helped collect the remaining bread when everyone was full. Jesus didn't want any of it to be wasted.

Well, give Philip his due here.
He did have a point.
There was no way that they would be able to get food for that size of crowd.
No way without Jesus, that is.

What are your 'no ways'?
No way you can provide something?
No way you can face something?
No way you can apologize for something?
No way you can forgive something?
No way you can exhibit grace in something?
No way you can move on from something?
No way you can . . .?

With Jesus, 'no way' does not need to have a full stop after it.
He turns it into 'no way . . . without me'.

Philippians 4:19:
'God will meet all your needs'.

He certainly met their needs that day!
The crowd must have been amazed as they all enjoyed the food.
And look who provided the food – Jesus.

But he didn't simply provide and then step back with a 'job done' attitude.
He stuck around to enjoy the blessing with the people.

Let's look at Zacchaeus, in Luke 19:
Jesus has been walking along.
He has been spotted by Zacchaeus, who had climbed a
tree so that he could get a better view of Jesus.
Actually, Zacchaeus has been spotted by Jesus.
And told to come down.
Zacchaeus, who no one likes, has actually been
acknowledged and publicly recognized by Jesus.
And, no doubt, Zacchaeus feels a whole lot better about
himself as he hurries down from that tree!

OK, Jesus might think, job well done.
Time to move on.
But, no.

Jesus then goes to Zacchaeus's house.
And spends time there with him.
Not because he has to, but because he wants to.
Jesus has just changed Zacchaeus's life from one of
loneliness and rejection to one of
inclusion and acceptance.
And that's exciting!
An excitement that Jesus wants to share.

When Jesus blessed the crowd by providing them with
food, he wanted to share in their enjoyment of it.
When Jesus blessed Zacchaeus by accepting him,
Zacchaeus was excited!
And Jesus stuck around to share that excitement.

When Jesus blesses you, he doesn't dash off as soon as the blessing happens.
No, he stays right there because he wants to share in the blessing.
Share in your enjoyment.
Share in your excitement.
Do you let him share it?

And Zacchaeus learned that Jesus doesn't put a full stop after blessings, any more than he does after 'no way'.
He just keeps the blessings coming.
Staying with Zacchaeus,
bringing salvation to his house . . .
You could say that the blessings were literally overflowing!

What's the first thing God did after he created people?
He blessed them (see Genesis 1:28).
He blessed us.
He blessed you.
And he has never stopped.

Notice that in the feeding of the 5,000, the disciples gathered up the leftovers.
They didn't want any of the blessing that Jesus had provided to go to waste.

Be someone who enjoys God's blessings, who gets excited by God's blessings, who looks for God's blessings, who doesn't put a full stop after God's blessings. Someone who doesn't let God's blessings go to waste.

Lord God,

Thank you that my 'no ways' don't have to be final.
You take the full stop away.
Help me to trust my 'no ways' to you.
And Lord, I am sorry for times when I take you and your blessings for granted.
Times when I am wasteful.
Please help me not to be.
Thank you that the blessings keep coming!

Amen

John's Jottings

Don't waste
God's blessings

My response:

Day 6

Well, I am on a writing roll here. All's well that ends well, I suppose, but this evening has been pretty scary.

After Jesus had fed the crowd, he told us to get in our boat and row across the lake while he went off by himself to pray for a bit. So we did. The water was calm enough when we set off, but it did not take long for a storm to blow up. That was OK, though – we are fishermen and used to dealing with storms. I don't think it was the storm that scared us so much as the ghost we saw walking on the water through the night. We were terrified. A ghost approaching us, stuck in the middle of a stormy lake with no idea of what to do . . . but then the ghost spoke and it wasn't a ghost after all. 'It's me. Don't be afraid.' And, suddenly, we weren't afraid any more. We let Jesus climb into the boat, the storm disappeared and we immediately found ourselves on the shore we'd been trying to row to.

Today must have been quite a day for the disciples! They'd seen Jesus feed the crowd, walk on water and calm a storm . . .

Let's think about the storm (see John 6:16–21):

Basically, the disciples have no idea what to do.
They are stuck in the middle of a storm.
They are terrified.
Their own efforts are getting them nowhere.

And suddenly, they see a ghost.
At least, they think it is a ghost.
They assume it is a ghost . . . but it's not.
It is Jesus.
Cue huge sighs of relief all round!

But, hang on a minute.
What has just happened here?
Jesus has been right there with the disciples.
They've been looking straight at him!
And yet, despite all the time they have spent with him recently, they didn't recognize him.

The disciples have let the storm change things.
They have allowed external circumstances to cloud and influence their perception of Jesus.

Let's look at Genesis 28:
Jacob is in trouble.
He has just tricked his father into giving him the blessing that was intended for his twin brother, Esau.
And now Esau is furious.
Furious enough to be making plans to kill Jacob.
So Jacob runs.

He gets away from there as fast as he can.
Imagine him, heart pumping wildly, constantly looking
over his shoulder to see if Esau is pursuing him . . .

Eventually he stops.
And starts thinking about his situation.
And his situation does not look good.
Not good at all.
Finally, Jacob falls into a troubled sleep.
And he dreams . . .

In his dream, he sees a ladder reaching up to heaven.
Standing at the very top of the ladder is the Lord.
Who basically says, 'I am with you.
And I'm not going anywhere.
So you'll be OK.'

Just as he says to you,
'I'm with you.
I'm not going anywhere.
So you'll be OK.'

When Jacob wakes up, and remembers the dream, he is
awestruck.
'Surely the Lord is in this place, and I was not aware of it'
(verse 16).

'Surely the Lord is in this place' – definitely true!
God is everywhere.

Psalm 139:8:

*'If I go up to the heavens, you are there;
if I make my bed in the depths, you are there.'*

'I was not aware of it' – that's true, too.
Jacob wasn't aware of it.

So the question is, why?
Why was Jacob not aware of God's presence?

Well, it seems that he was allowing all the bad things
that were happening in his life to prevent him from
recognizing God.
He was so busy focusing on what was going wrong that
he forgot that God had not gone anywhere.

He allowed his own fears and situation to supersede his
God.

Do you do that?
Permit circumstances to influence your perception of
God?
Or do you let God influence your perception of
circumstances?

The disciples discovered that with Jesus there, the storm
was not so bad after all.
But only when they recognized that he was there.

What about you, with the storms in your life?

Do you take time, in the midst of them, to recognize that God is there?

He says to you, (Hebrews 13:5 NLT):
'I will never fail you. I will never abandon you.'

God is there, you know.
He really is.

Lord God,

Thank you that you don't change.
That you are constant.
That you don't go anywhere.
Sometimes my perception of you does get mixed up.
Things go wrong.
I get scared.
I focus on my situation, rather than on you and who you are.
Help me to recognize you in my storms.
I want to be someone who expects you,
not someone who is surprised that you are there.

Amen

John's Jottings

Recognize
God

My response:

Day 7

We've been in Capernaum today. Jesus has been teaching in the synagogue. I have to say, he caused a bit of a stir. He was talking about how he's come down from heaven, and the people did not like that one bit. They know Jesus' parents, so how could he have come down from heaven? Then some of his disciples started grumbling. They said that Jesus' teaching that the only way to eternal life was through him was too hard for them to get their heads around. So lots of them gave up trying to 'get it' and stopped following Jesus. Jesus turned to the twelve of us core disciples and asked if we wanted to leave, too. We looked at each other in amazement and I think Peter summed up all our thoughts: 'Where else would we go? Who else would we follow?'

So, Jesus has been teaching.
And some of the Jews don't like what he is saying.
They don't like it when Jesus tells the truth. It's too hard.
They can't get their heads round it, and neither can many of the disciples.

So they give up.
They give up trying to understand.

What about you?
How do you handle truths from God?
Challenges from him?
Things that ask you to re-evaluate your life
and thinking?

Let's look at Mark 10:17–22:
Jesus is walking along when, suddenly, a man runs up to him.

This is unusual in itself.
A man would not have been caught running in those days.
Men wore long tunics and, in order to run, would have had to lift their tunics.
Which would show their bare legs.
Which, in that culture, was a demeaning thing to do.

But this man wanted to see Jesus more than he cared about doing the right thing in front of other people.

How about you?
Do you want to see Jesus more than you want to look good in the eyes of the world?

Paul wrote (in 1 Thessalonians 2:4):
'We are not trying to please men but God, who tests our hearts.'

Who do you try to please?

So, there is the man, now on his knees in front of Jesus, and he asks him a burning question:
'What do I need to do to get eternal life?'
And Jesus answers by listing some of the Ten Commandments.

At this, the man thinks he is OK.
He eagerly tells Jesus that he has never murdered, stolen etc.
In fact, he has kept the commandments ever since he was a young boy.
Phew, the man is probably thinking.
Looks like I am OK after all.
I live a good life.
I don't hurt anyone.
I don't lie, I don't cheat . . .

At this point, Jesus looks at the man and he loves him.
This out-of-breath, sweaty, self-confident, desperate, confused person
is looked at with love by Jesus.

Romans 8:39:
'[Nothing] will be able to separate [you] from the love of God'.

Nothing. At. All.

Then the man hears Jesus speaking again.
'There's still one thing missing.'

Huh? What could that be?

'Sell everything you have and give it to the poor.
If you do, you will have treasure in heaven.'

And the man's face falls.
He pictures his bank account.
It is looking healthy.
Very healthy.
As are his possessions.

He stands up, turns from Jesus and sadly walks away.
It's just too hard.

What is God asking of you?
How is he challenging you?
What is he asking you to re-evaluate in your life?

Will you try to understand why God is asking what he is
asking?
Jesus asked the man to sell his possessions on earth so
that he would have treasure in heaven.
Heaven is ahead!

Matthew 6:19–21:

*'Do not store up for yourselves treasures on earth,
where moth and rust destroy, and where thieves
break in and steal. But store up for yourselves
treasures in heaven, where moth and rust do not*

destroy, and where thieves do not break in and steal. For where your treasure is, there your heart will be also.'

Where is your heart?

Will you stick with God or will you be like some of the Jews, some of the disciples and the rich man, and just walk away?

Take on board Peter's words, 'Lord, where else would we go?'
Yes, your teaching is hard to understand,
you give us some tough home truths,
life is not always easy, but . . .
where else would we go?
Where else could we go?

Philippians 3:8 (NLT):

'Everything else is worthless when compared with the infinite value of knowing Christ Jesus my Lord.'

Day 7

Lord God,

Sometimes I find myself turning away.
Turning away from you.
I get tempted by other things.
By other feelings.
By other experiences.
But I don't want to.
I don't want to budge.
It just seems to happen.
I find things too hard ... and then I forget that not
being with you is harder still.
Everything really is worthless compared with you –
so help me to keep comparing!

Amen

John's Jottings

Stick with
Jesus

My response:

Day 8

Forgot to add this before; after Peter made it clear that we did not want to leave, Jesus said something puzzling. He said he's chosen us twelve, but one of us is a devil! I was so shocked at that that I put it out of my mind, but I've just been reminded of it as another dumbfounding subject has come up . . . Jesus has been talking about his own death. What? Jesus is going to die?? He's only in his thirties. He also talked about how he will suffer and will be rejected by the priests and teachers of the law. We were all stunned and Peter found his voice first (no surprise there!), telling Jesus to stop saying these things. But Jesus got angry at that. He said, and I quote, 'You do not have in mind the things of God, but the things of men.' Then he said that anyone who wants to truly follow Jesus must 'take up his cross'. And 'What good is it for a man to gain the whole world, yet forfeit his soul?'

I want to make sure I get all this down exactly – I definitely need to mull it over some more.

So, in a nutshell, Peter is telling Jesus to be quiet. He doesn't like what Jesus is saying so he wants to block it out and pretend it isn't happening.

Have you ever seen a child put their fingers in their ears if they don't like what someone is saying to them, trying to stop it being true?

That's what Peter is doing here.

Maybe you have done it yourself!

But what about spiritually?

Do you put your 'fingers in your ears' if you don't like what God is saying or doing?

Working on the childlike theory that if something is not heard then it will cease to be true?

Sometimes we can stop listening so abruptly that we miss out on the 'because' that inevitably follows hard teaching from God.

Let's look at Balaam, in Numbers 22:21–35:

Balaam is riding along on his donkey, when suddenly the donkey stops.

And turns off the road, into a field.

So Balaam hits her.

Next, the donkey squashes up close to a wall.

So Balaam hits her.

Then, when they are at a very narrow part of the road, with nowhere else to go,

the donkey lies down.

So Balaam hits her.

Balaam puts a full stop to the donkey's actions.

He does not like what the donkey is doing.

He's angry.
He wants to carry on with his journey, keep doing what he has been doing.
He's got his plans and he wants to stick with them.
So he does not bother to wonder why the donkey is behaving as she is.

Balaam is interested in the full stop, not the 'because'.

But it turns out that the 'because' is actually for Balaam's own good.
The donkey has seen the angel of the Lord, with a drawn sword, blocking their way.

Before Balaam sees the angel, the Lord enables the donkey to speak.
And she basically asks Balaam why he keeps beating her . . .
Hasn't she been his donkey for a long time?
And never done something like this before?
Why would she start now, unless there was a good reason?

Jesus could have said something similar to Peter.
Peter, haven't I been with you, day in, day out, for a while now?
Have I ever done or said anything that's not for your own good?
Why would I start now?

Just as God says to you,
'Haven't I been right beside you, every day of your life?
Haven't I always wanted the best for you?
Why would I stop wanting that now?'

After Peter tells Jesus to be quiet, Jesus says to him, 'You do not have in mind the things of God, but the things of men.' (Mark 8:33, see also, verses 34–37.)

Could the same be said of you?
Don't let human full stops get in the way of the things of God . . .
keep his ways at the forefront of your life and thinking.

Jeremiah 29:11:

' "I know the plans I have for you," declares the
*L*ORD, *"plans to prosper you and not to harm you,*
plans to give you hope and a future." '

'I know the plans I have for you . . .'
OK, stop right there. I have my own plans.
I know what I am doing – most of the time, anyway.
I'm not sure I'll like your plans, Lord, so let's just stop this conversation.
Right now.
Full stop.

'. . . plans to prosper you and not to harm you, plans to give you hope and a future.'
Oh.

OK.

I nearly missed that bit.

It looks as though your plans for me actually are the best.

May be better not to use full stops after all.

I don't want to miss the bit that follows . . .

Lord God,

I am sorry for the times when I turn away from you.

And put my fingers in my ears because I don't like what you are saying to me.

Or who you are challenging me to be.

Times when I use full stops.

I don't know why I forget that you want the best for me.

You always have,

so why would I think that you'd stop now?

Help me to be open to your leading . . .

Amen

John's Jottings

No full
stops

My response:

Day 9

Well, I have been doing lots of thinking but not much diary-writing this past week. Still haven't got my head around those things Jesus was saying, but have decided I will just have to trust him.

I have something amazing to write about today – Jesus went off up a mountain and took Peter, James and me with him. OK, I know that may not seem particularly amazing, but there's more . . . while we were up the mountain, Jesus changed. His face was shining and his clothes were as dazzling white as it is possible to be. Then two people appeared and began talking to him. They were Moses and Elijah! Peter started offering to put up shelters for the three of them, but was interrupted by a cloud. It was really bright and surrounded us all. Then a voice came from it, 'This is my Son, whom I love; with him I am well pleased. Listen to him!' Just like when Jesus was baptized. Peter, James and I were really scared and fell to the ground, but Jesus told us to get up and not be afraid. So we looked up and, when we did, saw no one but Jesus. Elijah and Moses had gone.

Jesus told us not to tell anyone what had happened. Not 'until the Son of Man has been raised from the dead', anyway. (See how I directly quote things I don't really understand?!) So I have not breathed a word, except to my diary . . .

So, John hears the voice from heaven again (Matthew 17:1–9), talking about Jesus.
And basically saying the same thing as last time – except for the added bit at the end:
'Listen to him!'
OK, this is who Jesus is – he is my Son, I love him, I am pleased with him . . .
So listen to him.

And God says this following Peter telling Jesus to be quiet. Jesus is there to be listened to, not silenced – so don't ignore him.

God was moving the disciples on in their knowledge of Jesus.
They knew he was God's Son, that God loved him, that God was pleased with him . . .
It was time for them to learn that Jesus was also someone worth listening to.

What about you?
How's your relationship with God at the moment?
Are you moving on in your knowledge?
Because there is always more to know.

The psalmist says, Psalm 42:2:
'My soul thirsts for God, for the living God.'

God is a living God!
A moving God . . .
Will you move with him?

The disciples here were moving with Jesus even though
they didn't know where they were going.
Or why they were having to struggle up a high
mountain.
What mattered was that Jesus didn't leave them behind.
And because they moved with him,
because they didn't decide that it would be easier to
stay at the bottom of the mountain,
they witnessed something amazing at the top.

All because they willingly moved
with Jesus.

Sometimes, let's be honest, we don't know where we
are going.
We are lost.
Aimless.
Confused.
Lacking in direction.

But it can still seem easier to stay at the bottom of the
mountain.
To stay with the familiar.

Let's look at David:
David was a shepherd boy.

The youngest in his family, he knew that he was way
down in the pecking order.

But at least he knew what he was doing.

Every day, he stayed out in the fields with the sheep.

Every day, he looked after and protected those sheep.

And David was good at what he did.

Then, one day, Samuel turns up.

Samuel is a prophet and has come on a mission from
God.

His mission is to anoint David as the next king of Israel.
David.

The shepherd boy.

King of Israel?

Leave his sheep? Leave all he knows? Leave what he is
confident in?

And for what? To be king?!

The thought has never even crossed David's mind . . .

And yet, he obeys.

He obeys God.

And he becomes one of the finest kings Israel
ever had.

Why did God choose David?

Talking about David, God said (Acts 13:22), 'I have
found David . . . a man after my own heart; he will do
everything I want him to do.'

Wow.
A man after God's own heart.
A man who wants what God wants.

And as we know from Psalm 42, God is living.
And if he is living and moving, anyone who wants to
follow his heart needs to move, too!
Needs to be a man or woman who chases after God's
heart.
Which is what David did.
The unknown future didn't matter because he knew the
God who was taking him into that future.

When God looks at you, can he say,
'I have found X . . .
Here is someone after my own heart'?

Someone who will move with me
Live with me
Change their plans for me
Step into the unknown for me
Take risks for me
Be the person I want them to be for me.
Someone who will trust their future to me . . . ?

Lord God,

I want to move with you.
I don't want to miss out because I am too scared.
Thank you that nothing is unknown to you.
Thank you that you found me.
Help me to listen to you.
To be someone you can look at and say,
'Here is a person after my own heart.'

Amen

John's Jottings

Chase God's
heart

My response:

Day 10

I am annoyed – why do people have to spoil things? It was such a fantastic experience to be up the mountain with Jesus, I wish we could have stayed there. Jesus really is someone special, why won't people see it?

We were travelling through Samaria and needed somewhere to stay the night. Now, I know Samaritans don't like Jews but this is not any Jew, this is Jesus! He sent messengers to ask if he could stay at someone's house, but the people refused. They basically said 'get lost'. And that made James and me really angry. Who did these people think they were? So we asked Jesus if he wanted us to call down fire from heaven and kill them all. But Jesus turned round and told us off, instead – that's all the thanks we got! Then we all just went to a different village.

John is well and truly back down from his mountain-top experience here.
He's just witnessed an amazing thing and has been really close to Jesus.
But now he's with people who don't realize how special Jesus is.
And that is annoying him, making him angry, igniting his temper.

How about you?
Do you realize how special Jesus is?
Maybe your quick answer is yes.
Of course I do.

But stop a minute and consider the question again:
Do you realize *how* special Jesus is?

Colossians 1:15–19:

'[Jesus] is the image of the invisible God, the first-born over all creation. For by him all things were created: things in heaven and on earth, visible and invisible, whether thrones or powers or rulers or authorities; all things were created by him and for him. He is before all things, and in him all things hold together. And he is the head of the body, the church; he is the beginning and the firstborn from among the dead, so that in everything he might have the supremacy. For God was pleased to have all his fulness dwell in him'.

Wow.

Maybe you are like John. You've met Jesus.
You realize how special he is.
Yet other people just don't seem to get it.
Why can't they see?
Maybe it doesn't make you want to call down fire from heaven (!), but it does make you want to shake them!

So there is John, wanting to annihilate these people,
and there is Jesus basically saying,
'Leave it. Let's move on.'

Sometimes, when we get angry with people,
when we disagree with them,
when they drive us up the wall,
the best thing to do is to take Jesus' advice:
leave it and move on.

Proverbs 29:11 (NLT):
*'Fools vent their anger, but the wise quietly hold
it back.'*

Ask God to help you be a wise person . . .

And not just wise in your relationships with others.
Ask him to help you be wise in your relationship with
yourself.

Don't beat yourself up – leave the past and move on.

Paul said, in Philippians 3:13,14:
'But one thing I do: forgetting what is behind and
straining towards what is ahead, I press on towards the
goal to win the prize for which God has called me
heavenwards in Christ Jesus.'

Paul had some pretty big stuff behind him to forget.
Persecuting Christians, for example (see Philippians 3:6).

But despite all that, he had something even bigger to focus on ahead:
A crown of righteousness (see 2 Timothy 4:8).

God is a God who makes your future so much bigger than your past.
So keep looking ahead.

And ask God to help you be wise in your faith.

2 Corinthians 13:5 (NLT):
'Examine yourselves to see if your faith is genuine.
Test yourselves.'

Do you do that?
Test yourself?
Give yourself a faith check?
See where you are on your journey with God?
Have you moved on since last week, last month, last year?
What are you doing to keep your relationship with him alive?
What is he saying to you?
What are you saying to him?
How's the conversation going?

A regular faith check will keep you spiritually alive!

Lord God,

Help me to stop and take stock sometimes.
Of other people.
Of me.
Of my relationship with you.
Thank you that you give me a big future –
help me to stop looking backwards.
Help me to look to you in everything I do.
Lord, you are my future – help me not to let other
things compete.
Help me to truly remember how special you are.

Amen

John's Jottings

Take a
faith check

My response:

Day 11

My mum turned up today. She just went straight up to Jesus and said she had something to ask him. So of course, Jesus stopped and asked her what she wanted. Talk about a shock when I heard what she said – she asked Jesus whether my brother James and I could sit either side of him in heaven! As if, I thought. Talk about presumptuous (though I have to admit, at the same time I was secretly a bit proud that she wanted that for us). Even Jesus told her that she did not understand what she was asking. Why is Mum embarrassing me like this?

I tried to just carry on walking but then Jesus turned to James and me. He asked us if we could drink the same cup that he would drink. And suddenly, I wasn't embarrassed any more. Of course I could, whatever the 'cup' was, and so could James. So we both said yes. But Jesus said that, actually, who sits where is not up to him anyway – God will sort that out. Which I thought would be the end of it, but the other disciples heard about our conversation and were really annoyed with James and myself. They thought we were trying to be the greatest, trying to be better than them. Then Jesus said something interesting. In his kingdom, the rules are different.

Day 11

On earth, everyone wants to be top dog but, Jesus said, the way to be really great is to serve other people. Interesting . . .

So, it is becoming clear that God's rules for living are very different from human rules for living.

Let's look at some of the rules that God gave Moses in the Ten Commandments (see Exodus 20):
Number eight – Don't steal.
Maybe you think that rule is not too bad.
You probably wouldn't break into someone's house and steal their TV.
You maybe wouldn't even slip some sweets into your pocket in a shop when no one was looking.

But what about another kind of stealing . . . stealing from God.
Do you sometimes steal from God?

Let's think about a way in which we can find ourselves stealing from God:

Wholeheartedness.

See 2 Chronicles 25 which talks about Amaziah, who had just become king of Judah.
Have a look at how it describes him in verse 2 (my italics):
'He did what was right in the eyes of the Lord, *but not wholeheartedly.*'

So, it seems that Amaziah went through all the motions of doing what God wanted.
He played the part very well.
But his heart just wasn't in it.
Well, not his whole heart, anyway.

He was maybe obeying God out of duty, habit, because it was the right thing to do . . .
Can the same be said of you?

'Wholeheartedly' means 'with total sincerity, enthusiasm, or commitment'
(collinsdictionary.com).
So, according to this, Amaziah was serving God insincerely, unenthusiastically and with a lack of commitment.
Can the same be said of you?

One day, not long after he became king, Amaziah decided to get an army together. He managed to get 300,000 men from Judah and then hired 100,000 men from Israel to join them. A sizeable army!

But then God sent a man with a message to Amaziah.
Basically, the men from Israel cannot go and fight with you.
If you take them, you'll lose.
And Amaziah's first response?
What about all that money that I paid for them?
Let's look at the reply:

'The Lᴏʀᴅ can give you much more than that.'

And he is still a God who can give you much more . . .
More than anything you can provide for yourself.
More than anything you can work out for yourself.
More than anything you can even imagine
(see Ephesians 3:20).

Because he is God and you're not.

Amaziah did as God said.
He sent the men from Israel away.
He went into battle without them.
And he defeated the Edomites.

Things might have been OK if the story had ended there.
But it didn't.

When Amaziah came back from battle, he brought with him the gods of the people he'd killed.
He bowed down before these gods and offered them sacrifices.

God sent another man to Amaziah, this time with a question:
'Why do you consult this people's gods, which could not save their own people?'

Why do you consult other gods?

Why do you turn to other places/people/things rather than God?
Why?

Isaiah 45:5:
*'"I am the L*ORD*, and there is no other;
apart from me there is no God."'*

Which leads us back to the Ten Commandments, and the very first one.
God says, 'You shall have no other gods before me.'
In other words: 'You must not let anything become more important than me.'

Are you obeying the commandment of the God who loves you enough to get jealous when other things take his place in your life (Exodus 34:14)?

Human rules say, look out for yourself.
God's rules say, let me look out for you.

Isaiah 46:4 (NLT):
*'I will be your God throughout your lifetime –
until your hair is white with age.
I made you, and I will care for you.
I will carry you along and save you.'*

Day 11

Lord God,

Your ways are not my ways.
I know that.
What I am not so good at remembering is that
your ways are the best.
At least, I am not good at living it.
I am not good at always being wholehearted in
following you.
I get distracted so easily.
I let other things take your place.
Help me to be constantly aware of this
so that I can stop it happening.
I want to live by your rules.
I choose to let you look out for me.

Amen

John's Jottings

God comes
first

My response:

Day 12

Yet another diary gap, sorry about this! A six-month break must be a diary-writer's record, but I am back now. We have been travelling around Galilee. Jesus stayed away from Judea because he knew that the people there wanted to kill him. But now it is time for the Feast of Tabernacles and Jesus' brothers have had a word with him. They basically said he should go to the feast. Lots of people would be there and Jesus' supporters could see him and hear about all the miracles he has been doing. To be honest, even Jesus' own brothers don't seem to realize how special he is. I find that strange, actually . . . Anyway, Jesus told them no, it was not his time yet, and that they should go on without him.

In the end, though, Jesus did go. He went secretly to Jerusalem. When he got there, people were whispering about him, wondering where he was. Some said that he was good, some that he was bad – it seems that opinion is divided when it comes to Jesus.

So, Jesus' brothers have appeared.
And they are trying to boss their brother about.
Trying to tell him what to do.

What about you?

Do you try to tell God what to do?

Try to tell him what the best course of action is?

Think that you know best?

Let's have another look at David (1 Samuel 17):

Before David actually became king, King Saul and the Israelite army were being threatened by the Philistines. The Philistines had a giant of a man, Goliath, and they challenged the Israelites to find just one man to fight him. But the Israelites were terrified.

They couldn't fight Goliath!

Until David came along.

And volunteered to go.

Saul summons David to see him.

When David arrives, Saul looks at him.

He looks him up and down.

And he reaches a conclusion:

'David, there is no way you can fight Goliath. You're just a boy. Goliath has years of fighting experience.'

David answers that he will be fine because God will be with him.

So Saul starts to come round to the idea.

If God is with David, then maybe it will be OK.

But I'd better tell God how to do it.

So Saul tries out his armour on David.

And it doesn't work.
David can't walk.
So David goes without it.
Without all the extra stuff that Saul thought was necessary . . .
And David is victorious.
Just as he'd said God would help him to be.

Not Saul's helmet.
Not Saul's armour.
God.
Saul may have done what he did with the best of intentions.
He didn't want things to go wrong, so he tried to prevent that from happening and, in doing so, he forgot that he was trying to tell God what to do.

God already knew the best course of action!
Because God is God.

Isaiah 55:8 (NLT):
'*"My thoughts are nothing like your thoughts," says the* LORD. *"And my ways are far beyond anything you could imagine."*'

Maybe Saul didn't *really* trust God.
Didn't *really* believe that God knew what to do.

Just as Jesus' brothers didn't *really* believe that he was someone special.

Didn't *really* trust him to be doing the best thing.
Even though they had known him all their lives.

What about you?
Maybe you have been journeying with God for a while.
Going to church, running activities, serving God in
various ways . . .
When you are so busy, so capable, do you remember to
remember that he knows best?
To check things out with him?
To trust him? *Really* trust him?
And do you remember to take time to recognize that he
is special?
To just stop and think 'wow'.

He says to you,
'Be still, and know that I am God' (Psalm 46:10).

Day 12

Lord God,

I'm sorry that I sometimes try to boss you around.
Through my words or my actions, I think I know
better than you.
How ridiculous.
Help me to trust you.
I mean, really trust you.
And Lord, don't let me lose sight of how special
you are.

Amen

John's Jottings

Let God be
God

My response:

Day 13

Halfway through the feast, Jesus decided to go public. He went to the Temple courts and began to teach the people. The Jewish leaders were absolutely flabbergasted at the things he said. They couldn't understand where Jesus had got all this knowledge from. They knew that he had not been through their prestigious education system and yet, here he was, teaching with the best of them! Jesus explained to them that what he said came directly from God, and that is how he was able to teach with such authority. I have to say, I'm not sure they were convinced by that, though. The chief priests and Pharisees even sent guards to arrest Jesus, that's how much they want to get rid of him. But the guards returned without him because they had never heard anyone speak as he did.

The leaders here seem to have backwards-facing binoculars!
They are so busy peering into the past that they miss the present.
They got so hung up on how they thought Jesus ought to behave that they missed out on how he actually was behaving.
So they tried to put Jesus in a box.

Do you do that?
Limit God by your own preconceptions?
Try to put him in a box that says, these are your limits?
Or, to take it one step further, a box that says:
'You can be God, but only within the boundaries I put in place?
Only when I am happy to let you be God'?
From everlasting to everlasting, God is God
(see Psalm 90:2).
Don't make him into a 'sometimes' God.

So, the Jews were so busy 'knowing' that there was no way Jesus should have all this knowledge that they missed out on what he was teaching them.
And what he was teaching them was he was the living water. That he could give them true life. Abundant life.

And he can do the same for you.
That's why he left heaven and came to earth!

John 10:10b (NASB):
[Jesus said,] 'I came that [you] may have life, and have it abundantly.'

Let's look at the Israelites, in Numbers 21:
The Israelites, led by Moses, are travelling through the desert.
It is quite a journey and they are getting fed up.
So they start complaining about anything they can think of – the desert, the lack of bread, the lack of water.

And they complain about Moses himself.
And God.
Blaming them for the current situation.

At this point, God decides that enough is enough, so he
steps in.
And he steps in by sending lots of poisonous snakes.
The snakes slither about among the people, biting them
as they go.
There was no escape and many of the people died.

And then Moses, who had been the target of the
people's frustration, prays for them.
What grace!
And how sensible.
Next time someone you know treats you unfairly,
rather than simmer and seethe, why not pray for them?
And, as Moses did, pray for their best.
You'll find it is hard to stay mad at someone who you are
asking God to bless!

So God tells Moses to make a snake out of bronze and
put it on a pole.
Anyone who had been bitten could look at the snake
and live.
And Moses delivers the message to the people.
A message that came straight from God.
Just as Jesus' words and teaching came directly from God.
Both Moses and Jesus 'spoke God' into the situations
around them – do you?

So, the people are left with a choice.
They know the snakes are there.
They can see them and feel them.
But what if they take their eyes off the snakes to look up
at the one on the pole?
That is a bit risky – how are they supposed to dodge the
snakes if they are not even paying attention to them?
OK, so God has told them to look up, but that really
does mean stepping outside the box! Doesn't seem
sensible at all . . .

But some of them decide to take the risk.
And they realize that it is not a risk at all – God is a
certainty, not a gamble.
And they are healed.
They received life.

Imagine how amazed they would have been.
And imagine how seeing their healings would have
encouraged others to let go of what they
thought they knew and *look*.

What about you?
Are you amazed by your God?
And does your amazement encourage others to 'let go
of what they know' and look to him?

Listen to God.
Believe in him.
Let go of what you 'know' and look.

Day 13

You say, 'I can't do this.'
He says, 'I will help you do it' (see Isaiah 41:10).

You say, 'I'm so alone.'
He says, 'No, you're not – I'm right here'
(see Deuteronomy 31:6).

You say, 'The future is scary.'
He says, 'Trust it to me' (Proverbs 3:5,6).

You say . . . ?
He says . . .

Lord God,

I am sorry that I try to limit you.
That I box you in.
I do it because I am scared.
Scared of not knowing.
But I know I have new things to know!
Help me to let go of what I think I know and to look to you.

Amen

John's Jottings

Let go
and look!

My response:

Day 14

Jesus spent last night on the Mount of Olives, just
outside of Jerusalem. But today he was back, teaching
the people in the Temple courts again.

The Pharisees are still lurking around, trying to
trap him into doing or saying something wrong.
Their latest trick was to bring a woman and make
her stand in front of Jesus and the group gathered
around him. The woman had been caught having an
affair and, as the Pharisees pointed out, the Law of
Moses states that she should be stoned to death. They
wanted to know what Jesus thought about that. But
Jesus turned the tables on them. He basically said,
OK – whoever has never committed a sin, any sin
at all, is the one that can throw the first stone. And
no one threw a stone. One by one, all the crowd went
away.

I looked back and there was only Jesus left,
standing there with the woman.

Here we have a woman being dragged before a crowd
(John 8:2–11).
Imagine the scene:
An embarrassed and guilty woman.
Gloating Pharisees.

A crowd of onlookers, mouths open at what they are witnessing.
And Jesus.

Jesus, who said to the woman, 'I don't condemn you.'

Jesus, who says to you, 'I don't condemn you.'

Psalm 103:12 (NLT):
*'He has removed [y]our sins as far from [you]
as the east is from the west.'*

Let's look at Paul, in 2 Timothy 4:
Paul is nearing the end of his life.
He is stuck in prison, facing trial.
Maybe, as he sits there, he thinks of his friends –
will they come to visit him?
And Paul realizes that the answer is 'no'.
All his friends desert him.

In fact, at Paul's first trial, not one person came to his support.
Not one.
Paul was all alone.
And what did Paul have to say about this situation?
No one was there for me.
No one was there. . . . 'But the Lord stood at my side and gave me strength' (verse 17).

Paul wasn't on his own – the Lord was with him.

84

The woman wasn't alone – Jesus stayed with her.
And you don't need to be alone, either:

Psalm 46:1:
*'God is [y]our refuge and strength,
an ever-present help in trouble.'*

You have a God who not only walks in when the rest of
the world walks out, but a God who says,
'I am here to stay.
I'm not going anywhere.'

And so, one at a time, the crowd left.
They knew they weren't perfect.
Eventually, there was just Jesus and the woman,
standing there alone.

Note that John includes himself amongst those who
had to walk away.
He did not think himself a cut above the rest of them.

Let's look at the parable Jesus told about a Pharisee and
a tax collector in Luke 18:
The parable is set in the Temple.
A Pharisee and a tax collector are there.
And they are praying.
The Pharisee basically thanks God that he is far superior
to other men.
That he is not as bad as robbers and adulterers.
He's not even as bad as the tax collector over there.

He fasts twice a week and gives away a tenth of his
income.
Amen!

The tax collector, on the other hand, prays just one line:
I know I am a sinner. Please, God, have mercy on me.
Amen.

And Jesus praised the tax collector:
'Everyone who exalts himself will be humbled, and he
who humbles himself will be exalted' (verse 14).

John didn't think he was better than other people.
Neither did the tax collector.
The Pharisee did, though.
Which one are you like?
Remember which man Jesus praised . . .

So, we have a God who sticks around.
But more than that, we have a God who is sometimes
the only one *able* to stick around.
No one in the crowd could have stayed, because none
of them were able to say that they'd never sinned.
But Jesus could. And he did.

Sometimes, people do not know how to deal with things.
So they walk out.
Or things become difficult.
So they walk out.
They just can't stay.

They're not able to.
And maybe we feel as though we are left alone.

Remember the Transfiguration, when Jesus went up a mountain and was joined by Moses and Elijah?
The disciples, from their position on the ground, looked up and 'saw only Jesus' (Matthew 17:8 NLT).
Paul, after being deserted and left alone, knew that nevertheless Jesus was right there beside him.
The woman, after being accused, bullied, humiliated, abused, abandoned . . . experienced someone who stayed.

Have you experienced 'someone who stays'?

Zephaniah 3:17:
'The LORD your God is with you'.

Lord God,

You don't condemn me.
Wow.
You don't condemn me, even when I condemn myself.
When I beat myself up about things.
And more than that, you stay with me.
Thank you that you will never let me down.
Help me to keep looking up.
To look up and see you.

Amen

John's Jottings

Jesus stays
with me

My response:

Day 15

Jesus has carried on teaching in the Temple for the
last few days. Some of the Jews are really against
him; they don't like what he is saying at all. They
especially don't like him saying that he has come
from God. In the end, they were so angry that they
actually picked up stones to throw to kill him. But
Jesus just hid and then slipped away from the Temple.

Later, we were walking along when we saw a man
who had been blind from birth. We disciples asked
Jesus who had sinned. Well, of course someone must
have sinned if the man had been born blind, that's
what the rabbis teach. Except Rabbi Jesus, it would
seem. Jesus said that the man had been born blind not
because anyone had sinned, but so that his life could
show God at work. Then, before our very eyes, Jesus
spat on the ground and made a sort of muddy paste
from the dust. He put it on the man's eyes and told
the man to go and wash it off . . . and the man could
see!

When his friends and neighbours saw the man,
apparently they didn't think it was really him, they
thought it was a lookalike or something. He tried to
convince them that it was him and that Jesus had
healed him, but the people were still cynical. They

wanted to know where Jesus was, but the man did not know . . .

Why? Why me? What did I do to deserve this?
It is a common question and one that most of us will have asked, either for ourselves or on behalf of someone else.
It is also a question that has been around for a long time.
David famously asked it:

Psalm 22:1 (NLT):
'My God, my God, why have you abandoned me?'

Why, God? Why?! Where are you? What's going on?
And the silence is deafening.

Fast-forward hundreds of years to the events in today's diary entry.

The disciples ask (John 9:2): 'Who sinned . . . that [this man] was born blind?'
Basically, why did this happen to him?
Why can't he see?
Why?
What's going on?

And this time, there is an answer.
Jesus answers.
'So that the work of God might be displayed in his life.'

The disciples assumed that what was happening to the man must be some sort of punishment.
Retribution for something he or his parents had done.
But Jesus categorically refutes that.
Bad stuff happening, he says, does *not* automatically mean a person is being punished.
And the same is true today.
When you go through tough times, don't make them even harder.
Don't punish yourself by assuming that God is punishing you.

'So that the work of God might be displayed in his life.'

Think about it.
We have a God who is at work, everywhere.
And his work needs to be displayed.
Through other people.
Through this blind man. Through you.

The blind man could not hide the fact that Jesus had been at work in his life.
It was there for all to see!

Is God's work being displayed through you?
Through how you live, how you react, what you say –
In good times and bad?

God made you to reflect his glory.
You are his masterpiece (Ephesians 2:10 NLT).

He made you and is so proud of what he made that he put his signature on you.
He says, 'Hey, world; look what I made!'

Just as he puts his signature on things he wants to do through you.
A signature that is always there.
A signature that says, however tough things get, whatever you have to deal with, we're in this together.

Do you hide God's signature or do you have it on display?
Have it acknowledging who is at work in you, through you, enabling you?
Letting it display the work of God in your life?

But even if we do not deliberately hide God at work, we can sometimes forget to actively display him.

Take the man in today's diary entry.
One minute he is blind, the next minute he can see!
And all because of Jesus.
All because Jesus helped him.
But what happens next?
How does the man answer when people ask where Jesus is?
'I don't know.'

The man had been in a fix, accepted help from Jesus, and then seemingly just gone on his way.

Gone home, not appearing to give Jesus a second thought.
Does that ring a bell with you?
Turn to God when things get tough and then, when he has sorted them, forget about him until the next time you are in a spot of trouble?

'I don't know.'

How would you answer?
What would you say if someone asked you where Jesus is?

Maybe you sometimes feel that you don't know?
You look at what's going on around you, or at what's going on inside you, and think, where's God in all this?

Isaiah 43:1,2 (NLT):
'Do not be afraid, for I have ransomed you. I have called you by name; you are mine.
When you go through deep waters, I will be with you. When you go through rivers of difficulty, you will not drown. When you walk through the fire of oppression, you will not be burned up; the flames will not consume you.'

That's where God is.
Right there with you.

That tough situation? God's there.
The turmoil going on inside you? God's there.

The confusion and worry you can't get rid of? God's there.
The feeling of inadequacy that you carry? God's there.
The dread of tomorrow? God's there.
Whatever it is, God's there.

So you don't need to say 'I don't know' where God is.
Because you know.

Lord God,

Thank you that you answer my questions.
Actually, thank you that you are the answer to my questions!
Thank you that you put your signature on me –
help me to let it show.
And Lord, I never want to have to say I don't know where you are.
Help me to stick with you.
Help me to always know that you are right there with me.

Amen

John's Jottings

I <u>know</u> where
Jesus is

My response:

Day 16

We received a message today. Well, Jesus did. The message came from Mary and Martha, sisters of Lazarus. The family are good friends of ours. But now Lazarus is ill. That's what the message was, and Mary and Martha obviously wanted Jesus to go and heal Lazarus. But when he got the news, Jesus stayed where he was for a few more days before saying, 'OK, let's go.'

We disciples thought about that and were not sure it was a very good idea – yes, Lazarus was ill, but Lazarus was also in Judea and Judea is where the people tried to stone Jesus not so long ago. Jesus was determined, though, and in the end we decided that we may as well go. We would die with him, if necessary.

When we got there, we were told that Lazarus had died. He had passed away four days ago. I think Martha had a point when she told Jesus that if Jesus had been there sooner, Lazarus would not have died. But she also had a point when she said that, even now, God would give Jesus whatever he asked . . . and she was right. Jesus told Lazarus to come out of the grave – and he did. Lazarus is alive and well!

Jesus wept.
That's what the Bible tells us.
When Jesus saw how upset Mary was, he was troubled
and, when he arrived at the grave of Lazarus,
he wept (John 11).
For himself?
For the family?
For others?

Quite possibly all of the above, but the point is,
Jesus wept.
He knew what it was like to feel emotions,
to find things hard,
to be faced with a situation that upset him,
to need a good cry . . .

He understands.

We will go through difficult times.
We will find things tough.
But we can choose to go through them with one who
understands right beside us.

He's willing to walk with you,
he wants to walk with you –
but whether or not you let him walk with you is your
choice.
Will you let him?

Jesus said,

Matthew 11:29:
*'"Take my yoke upon you and learn from me, for I
am gentle and humble in heart, and you will find
rest for your souls."'*

Mary and Martha were experiencing pain.
Their beloved brother was ill, they knew that Jesus
could help, so they sent for him . . . and he didn't come.

Let's look at this from Jesus' point of view:
Jesus receives a message to say that his friend is ill.
He knows that people are expecting him to help.
And he knows that he can help.
He could go and heal Lazarus, right now.
And God would be praised.

But Jesus also knows that if he waits, God will ultimately
be even more glorified.
Yes, it will mean people will hurt,
be bewildered and struggling,
know heartache,
suffering,
confusion . . .
but a delay will also mean more glory for God.
And what does Jesus decide?
He decides that the more glory God receives, the better
. . . and so Jesus delays.

Delays can be tough. We want answers now!
But delays can also be God-glorifiers.

God knows what he is doing;
It's our job to trust what he is doing.

God says, in Isaiah 55:9 (NLT):
'Just as the heavens are higher than the earth, so my
ways are higher than your ways and my thoughts higher
than your thoughts.'

So, eventually Jesus arrives.
And he is greeted by Martha:
'Lord, if you had been here, my brother would not have
died.'
Then Mary comes along:
'Lord, if you had been here, my brother would not have
died.'

Identical words from the sisters, but there is a
difference –
Mary's speech ends there,
Martha's doesn't.

Mary basically says,
You should have been here.
But you weren't.
And so Lazarus is dead.
End of story.

Martha, however, adds a 'but' after her statement;
'But I know that even now God will give you whatever
you ask.'

Mary is closing the door on God because her mind cannot see a way out of her situation.
She's forgetting that God's thoughts are higher.

Easy to do, isn't it?

Martha, on the other hand, despite grappling with the same situation, is able to say,
'I don't get this.
I am confused.
I am hurting.
But God is still God.'

She leaves the door open for God to work.

Job, despite all the suffering he was going through (see the book of Job), was able to say (19:25),
'I know that my Redeemer lives'.
I know it.
I may not feel it right now, but I know it.

Job left that door open, put his hand through it and clung on to God.
So did Martha.
Can you add, 'So do I'?

Day 16

Lord God,

Thank you for your heart.
A heart that was troubled when you saw Mary going through a tough time.
A heart that is troubled when I go through tough times.
A heart that cries with me and stays with me.
Father, help me not to push you away.
Help me to trust you in delays.
Let me remember that you are God.
To leave a door open for you.
And to reach through and hold on.

Amen

John's Jottings

Leave the
door open

My response:

Day 17

I was going to say that we are heading towards Jerusalem, but that may be the wrong way to put it. It implies just walking along, normally. I really should learn that 'normal' rarely happens when Jesus is around!

We started walking but then, as we got near to Jerusalem, Jesus sent two of us to get a donkey from a village nearby. His instructions were to untie the donkey and bring it to him. Just make off with someone's donkey?! But simply saying 'The Lord needs this donkey' was enough, as Jesus had said it would be. Jesus climbed on and off we went. And it was not long before we were met by a massive crowd. They were in Jerusalem and had heard that Jesus was on his way. They were shouting and cheering and singing and dancing. They threw branches on the ground for the donkey to walk on. I don't know if anyone else was confused, but I was – I thought these people had been told to report Jesus, not welcome him? If they had, they were not obeying – the Pharisees are despairing and Jesus is more popular than ever!

So, two disciples are sent to get a donkey.
Actually, they are sent to go and take a donkey that

belongs to someone else.
Bit of a strange thing to be asked to do, but it was OK,
because Jesus told them what to say.

Sometimes, we find ourselves in strange situations.
Situations where we are not sure what to say, what to
think, how to act.

In Matthew chapter 10, Jesus' disciples were anticipating
some challenging situations, and what did Jesus say to
them?

Verse 19 (NLT):
'Don't worry about how to respond or what to say. God
will give you the right words at the right time.'

And he says the same to you.
Don't worry about it – I'm here to help.
'At the right time.'
Not necessarily when and how you want it, but
definitely when and how you need it.

Peter and John find the donkey and, following instructions,
untie it and tell the owner that the Lord needs it.
Which is enough for the owner.
He does not even ask why.

Is 'The Lord needs it' (Luke 19:31) enough for you?
With your money? With your time?
With your talents?

With your commitments?
With your dreams?
With your future?

If the Lord needs them, will you 'untie them and bring them to him'?
Will you let go of keeping them for your own good,
for your own use,
for your own achievements?
Without necessarily asking why, but just because the Lord needs them?

And will you also untie other things:
your past . . .
your worries . . .
your guilt . . .
your anger . . .
your shame . . .
your secrets . . .

Because God wants you to let go of those things, too.
He has set you free from them!

Galatians 5:1:
'It is for freedom that Christ has set [you] free.'

You've been set free – can you tell?

So, Jesus gets on the donkey and rides along, greeted by a cheering crowd.

They are excited to see him.
They are celebrating.
And they have been told to report him, so that Jesus can be arrested.
The people are not doing as they have been told, that's for sure!

Let's look at Luke 18:35–42:
A man is sitting by the road.
He is begging.
And he is blind.
He hears a crowd gathering around him, chatting excitedly.
And he realizes that Jesus is on his way.
Jesus, who everyone is talking about.
Jesus, who has been healing people and performing miracles.
Jesus, who might be able to help him.

So the man calls out, 'Jesus, help me!'
And the crowd tell him to be quiet.
But the man shouts all the louder, 'Jesus, help me!'
And Jesus does.
And the man can see again.

What if the man had obeyed the people in the crowd?
He would have missed out on what Jesus could offer him.
What if the crowd who welcomed Jesus had obeyed the religious leaders who told them to report him?

They would have missed out on being able to celebrate with Jesus.

What if you obey people who tell you the 'right way' to come to God, or not to come to him at all?
People who tell you how you should be responding to him?
What will you miss out on?
Or maybe you even tell yourself how you should be responding.
Listening to your mind, your background, tradition – and ignoring your heart.
Even when, like the blind man, your heart urges you to cry out.

Psalm 27:8:

'My heart says of you, "Seek his face!"
*Your face, L*ORD*, I will seek.'*

The crowd welcoming Jesus and the blind man both responded to the Jesus they were getting to know rather than the Jesus they had been told about.

Do you respond to what you know or to what you have been told?
What is your heart saying to you?
Will you listen?

Lord God,

Thank you that you have set me free.
Help me to untie things in my life and bring them to you.
And please use them and me as you want to.
For your glory.
Lord, I want to get to know you now.
Every day.
Help me to move with you and keep getting to know you better.
I will seek your face.

Amen

John's Jottings

Seek God's
face

My response:

Day 18

I'm not sure I understand Jesus sometimes. Things are going well, he's really popular, and now he is talking about his death. I know he has talked about it before, but the difference this time is that he is saying that the time for his death is now. I don't think he is looking forward to it but he is not avoiding it, as he has done when people have tried to kill him in the past. I'd better copy out word for word what he actually said: 'Now my heart is troubled, and what shall I say? "Father, save me from this hour?" No, it was for this very reason I came to this hour. Father, glorify your name!' and a reply came from heaven, 'I have glorified it, and will glorify it again.' I have mixed feelings right now – I am dreading what's to come but, at the same time, am reassured by God's voice . . .

Jesus is finding things hard and yet he says, in effect, that he is not going to give up (John 12:27,28).
That there is a reason for the stuff that is happening to him.
A reason that this time has arrived.

Let's look at Joseph, in the book of Genesis:

Joseph has been going through some ups and downs lately.

His brothers thought about killing him but decided to sell him into slavery instead.

So he was carried off to a foreign land.

He has spent time in prison after being falsely accused by his boss's wife.

But now he has risen to be the second most important person in the whole land.

He is in charge of managing the food crisis to make sure that people survive the famine.

People are travelling for miles, from different countries, to buy food from Joseph.

And then, one day, his brothers turn up, wanting to buy food.

They don't recognize Joseph, but he recognizes them.

And in the end, after quite a while, he tells them who he is.

And they are horrified!

Surely Joseph will kill them now?

Surely he will be out for revenge?

But what does Joseph say?

Genesis 50:20:

'You intended to harm me, but God intended it for good to accomplish what is now being done, the saving of many lives.'

You intended to harm me but God intended it for good . . .

It was a bad situation, but there was a reason I 'came to this hour'.

Do you look for reasons in the timings in your life?
Whether big things, little things, happy things, sad
things, do you ask yourself,
Why has God put me here right now?
What can I do for him?
What's his intention?
Is there a reason I have come to this hour?

So, bad stuff is happening . . . and yet God speaks.
John hears God's voice.
In the midst of all that is going on,
all the confusion,
all the worry,
God speaks.
'I have glorified [my name], and will glorify it again.'
Basically, God seems to be saying, glorifying is my
business, it is what I do!
So I am going to keep doing it.

What else does God say, in the midst of the rollercoaster
of life?
What else is his business?

Peace (John 14:27)
Presence (Joshua 1:5)
Joy (Psalm 16:11)
Strength (Psalm 46:1)
Guidance (Proverbs 3:5,6)
Love (John 3:16)
Acceptance (Isaiah 55:1)

Do you take time to hear him speak these words into your busy-ness?
Time to stop listening to everything but him?
Time to be reassured by God's voice?

He never stops speaking.
Can you say that you never stop listening?

Lord God,

When things are tough, thank you that you are there.
When I come upon times and situations, good or bad, help me to do so with you.
To remember to ask, 'Why am I here right now? What is your intention?'
And I need to learn to listen to the answer.
To listen to everything else you say to me, too.
Help me to keep listening . . .

Amen

John's Jottings

Keep
listening

My response:

Day 19

It is nearly time for the Passover feast now and we were all together, having a meal, when Jesus did something totally unexpected. He got up and started washing our feet! What? Why was Jesus doing the job of one of the servants? Most of us kept our confusion to ourselves and just let Jesus get on with it. Peter, unsurprisingly, didn't.

When Jesus got to Peter, Peter refused point-blank to have his feet washed. The rest of us looked at each other, then back at Peter. He was still refusing. Then Jesus told him that if he did not have his feet washed, he would have nothing to do with Jesus. Of course, Peter being Peter then went the other way and told Jesus to wash his head and hands as well. Talk about going over the top.

Now Judas has disappeared. Jesus told him to go and do whatever he was going to do, and to do it quickly. I am not sure what that meant but anyway, Judas has still not come back. And Jesus is still saying that he himself will not be with us for much longer . . . our group seems to be fragmenting.

Peter goes from one extreme to the other.
One minute he is refusing to let Jesus even wash his feet

and the next he is wanting his head and hands washed as well.

What brought about this change?

Well, Peter realized.

He realized that he'd be separated from Jesus.

He grasped the consequences of refusing – and he didn't like them.

He didn't like them one bit.

Sometimes, like Peter, we want to say no to God.

We don't understand what he is doing.

Or, maybe we understand the what but not the why.

We don't see why he wants to do what he wants to do in our lives.

Why exactly did Peter refuse?

Maybe he was embarrassed.

His feet would have been hot and sweaty and dirty and smelly from all the walking on dusty roads.

Letting Jesus wash them would mean letting Jesus near them.

Letting Jesus touch them.

Letting Jesus close to the worst part of him.

And Peter wasn't sure he wanted to do that.

Let's look at Adam and Eve:

The first people ever.

Created by God.

Given a beautiful place to live.

Only one thing they are not allowed to do –

Eat from a certain tree.
But that's OK.
There are loads of other trees to eat from.
It's not as if they will go hungry!

But in the end, the temptation is too great.
Adam and Eve eat fruit from the forbidden tree.
And when they do, they realize that they are naked.
Which makes them embarrassed. So they hide.
They hide from God.

That evening, God walks in the garden as usual.
But, this time, there is no one to greet him.
So God asks, 'Adam, where are you?'

Where are you? How sad.
Adam had moved away from God . . .
If he hadn't, God would not have needed to ask the question.

Does God need to ask that question of you?
Where are you?
Have you moved away from him?
Where are you?

God says, in Jeremiah 15:19 (NLT):
'If you return to me, I will restore you'.

Adam answers God,
'I am hiding because I am naked.'

Basically, I don't want you to see me like this.
Just as Peter didn't want Jesus anywhere near his feet.

Before he ate the fruit, Adam had no problem with
being naked in God's presence.
In fact, Genesis 2:25 says that Adam and Eve 'were both
naked, and they felt no shame.'

What about you?
Can you stand before your God, with your whole life on
display, and say that you feel no shame?
In the things you think, do, say . . . ?

Psalm 51:10:
'Create in me a pure heart, O God.'

Jesus told Peter that he needed access to Peter's feet,
unless Peter wanted nothing more to do with him.
In a sense, Jesus needed access to the bad things in
order to continue their relationship.
And Peter decided that being close to Jesus was more
important than hiding the bad stuff from him.
And so he let Jesus wash his feet.

Do you let Jesus wash your feet?
Wash the bad stuff?
Have access to the things within you that no one else
knows about?
Or is hiding them more important than letting Jesus in?

Jesus knelt before Peter.
Jesus took Peter's feet in his hands.
Peter's dirty, smelly feet . . .
Jesus took them in his hands – and wiped them clean.

And he can do the same for you.

Isaiah 1:18 (NLT):
*'"Come now, let's settle this,"
says the LORD.
"Though your sins are like scarlet,
I will make them as white as snow.
Though they are red like crimson,
I will make them as white as wool."'*

Come . . .

Lord God,

*Peter is not the only one to feel embarrassed
before you.
I sometimes do.
I feel embarrassed about the bad stuff.
And Lord, there is a lot of bad stuff.
Help me to come to you.
I want our relationship to move on.
Please wash me clean.*

Amen

John's Jottings

Come

My response:

Day 20

I think Jesus must have sensed that we were all feeling a bit unsure after Judas didn't come back and then being told that Jesus himself would not be around for much longer. So he told us not to worry but to trust in God. Don't worry?! Well, I am sure we will do our best with that one, though I think it is easier said than done. But, again, Jesus knew our thoughts. He went on to say that when he went, he would leave his peace behind with us. His very words were 'my peace I give you'. And he was talking to us, to me. He gives his peace to me!

Now I think about it, I don't think I have ever been as at peace as I have during the past three years I've spent with Jesus. I used to have such a temper and now I have peace. I know which I prefer! It's good to know that the peace will not be taken away . . .

'Don't worry' is one of those things that is easy to say but often hard to do, isn't it?
We live in a world that is full of people who are good at worrying.
And that world has been around for a long time.
Let's look at a poor widow, 1 Kings 17:

This widow has no food.
But she wants some.
She wants some very badly.
And she is worried about how she will manage to get some.
Along comes the prophet Elijah.
Who tells the widow to use up some of her last ingredients in making him something to eat.
Him, not her.
Because God told Elijah that she'd feed him.
And that it will be OK.
So the woman does.
And it was OK – she did not run out of food, God just kept providing more.

Let's apply this story to the question of peace.

The widow is worrying about what to do, how to do it, how to get herself out of the mess she is in.
Sound familiar?

She needs some food but does not have any.
Can't find any.
Does not know where to start resolving this situation.
Do you need peace but don't have any?
Can't seem to find any, no matter how hard you look?
Don't know where to start?

Then Elijah comes along and tells the woman what to do.

He tells her where to find food.
A bit like Jesus in today's diary entry, telling the disciples where they could find peace.
Just as he continues to do today.

'My peace I give you' (John 14:27).

Think about it.
Jesus says to you, 'I give you my peace.'

In Isaiah 9:6, Jesus is referred to as the 'Prince of Peace'.

What does it mean to have peace?
It means no more turmoil.
No more fretting.
No more worrying.

That's what Jesus offers you when he offers you his peace.
That's what he wants to give you – will you take it?

And then, despite using her ingredients, the widow doesn't run out of food.
Or maybe she didn't run out *because* she used her ingredients.

She could have been so afraid of losing what she had that she decided not to use it at all.
Decided to hang on to it.
So it would have just stayed there, neither use nor ornament.

Maybe you are afraid to tap into peace at all.
You think it is too good to be true.
You worry about what will happen if you stop worrying.
If you stop trying to do it all by yourself.
If you stop being in control.
So peace just sits there, like the widow's ingredients could have done.
Within your sights.
Full of untapped potential.

As we take hold of God's peace, we are able to receive more and more.
But we need to take hold of it, every day.

Let's look at the Israelites, in Exodus 16:
God provided food for them.
Every day.
But some thought that they should store it up.
Just in case food did not arrive tomorrow.
And they found that didn't work.
The food went mouldy.
They were trying to live on food that God had provided for another day.
Forgetting that God provides food for today.

Do you do that with peace?
Forget that God provides every day?

'His mercies begin afresh each morning'
(Lamentations 3:23 NLT).

And then, when you do forget, do you try to use leftover peace? Memories of peace?
Man-made peace . . . and it doesn't really work?

Every day, God gives you a present.
A peace-present.
It's up to you whether you open it.
It won't look the same each time.
But it will be just right for now.

John 14:27:

' "Peace I leave with you; my peace I give you.
I do not give to you as the world gives. Do not let
your hearts be troubled and do not be afraid." '

Open your present and find God's peace for you today.
A peace that nothing and no one can take away.

Lord God,

Being full of worry is easy for me.
Being full of peace is not.
Thank you that it is the other way round with you!
And thank you for your gifts – help me to open my peace-present every day.
Not just open it but use it, too.
Help me not to let anyone or anything take it away.

Amen

John's Jottings

Open my
peace present

My response:

Day 21

I think something is really about to happen now. I can feel the tension and Jesus is saying that the time has come. Has, not will. I am not really sure exactly what time has come. I am sure that it is not going to be easy, though. But right now Jesus has just finished praying and I want to record some of what he prayed.

He prayed specifically for his disciples, for people that follow him. He asked God to protect us. Not protect us by removing us from the world and its problems, but by protecting us from the devil while we are still in the world. He said that just as God sent Jesus into the world, Jesus is sending us. He asked that we may 'have the full measure of his joy' within us. Wow. Jesus has to be one of the most joy-full people I have ever met! He prayed more, too. I am amazed that Jesus would talk to God about me . . .

How joyful are you?
And let's be clear, joyful is not the same as happy.
It is possible to feel absolutely down in the dumps and yet still know joy.
Know joy deep down inside.
Because God is there.

Habakkuk 3:17,18 (NLT):
'Even though the fig trees have no blossoms,
*   and there are no grapes on the vines;*
even though the olive crop fails,
*   and the fields lie empty and barren;*
even though the flocks die in the fields,
*   and the cattle barns are empty,*
yet I will rejoice in the LORD!
*   I will be joyful in the God of my salvation!'*

Even though bad stuff is happening, I will rejoice in the Lord.
And that's the key.

No one is saying to be joyful about terrible situations.
Instead, be joyful in the Lord despite those situations.
God is the eye of the storm.
When things are raging, difficult, going wrong – he is in the midst.
He doesn't change.
He is right there.
And he is always still a God to be joyful in.

Check your focus . . .

Let's look at Peter, in Matthew 14:22–32:
Peter, bold, impulsive, daring, is walking on water.
In the middle of a storm.
He is walking towards Jesus.
He has his eye on his goal and all is well.

But suddenly, Peter starts to think about what he is doing.
He thinks about the storm raging.
He thinks about the fact that there is no solid ground under his feet.
And thinking leads to looking.
He looks at the storm and, as a result, he stops looking at Jesus.
And he begins to sink.

Sometimes, we can think too much.
And, when we do, it's possible that we put our perspective on a situation.
And push out God's perspective.

God's perspective in the storm was,
Hey Peter, it's OK. I'm right here.
Yes, the storm is raging but keep looking at me and you'll be just fine.
Focus on me, not on the storm.

Peter's perspective was, Oh no! Look at that storm!

When Peter first set off, walking on water, he knew amazement,
excitement,
joy.
Despite the storm.
Because Jesus was there.

When Peter started sinking, he knew
terror,
fear,
desperation.
Because of the storm.
Despite the fact that Jesus was there.

Because Peter forgot to look to Jesus!

What about you?
During the storms in your life?
Where do you focus?
On the storm . . . or on the God who is in the midst of it?
The God who offers you the ability to get through it.
To walk on water
if you focus on him.
And that's just the start.

God not only offers you the ability to get through the
storm.
He says that, with him, you can do so with joy.

Psalm 16:11 (NASB):
'In [God's] presence is fullness of joy'.

Remember; when Jesus prayed the prayer he prayed in
today's diary entry,
he was praying it for you.
He was asking God to protect you.

And that protection alone is enough to fill you to
overflowing with joy.
Or at least it should be.
Are you overflowing?
Do you know the 'full measure of [his] joy' (John 17:13)?

Psalm 63:7 (NLT):
*'Because you (God) are my helper,
I sing for joy in the shadow of your wings.'*

Lord God,

Thank you for sharing your joy.
And your protection.
*Help me to know them, even in the storms, and
never let them go.*
Let my joy overflow!

Amen

John's Jottings

Know
joy

My response:

Day 22

Well, something has happened now. Jesus has been arrested and taken to the high priest. After Jesus had finished praying for us, we all moved on to the Mount of Olives. He told the other disciples to sit down while he went off to pray, but he took Peter, James and me with him. Jesus told the three of us that he was really struggling and that he was going a bit further on, to be on his own. But he asked us to stay where we were and watch with him. He wanted some solidarity, I guess. And I am ashamed to write what happened next – the three of us fell asleep.

Jesus came back, woke us up and asked us again to keep watch . . . but we fell asleep again. The next time Jesus woke us, it was to say that his betrayer was on the way. I looked and could hardly believe my eyes (and I wasn't dreaming) – Jesus' betrayer was Judas! He avoided eye contact with us and just went straight up to Jesus. He kissed him, which was obviously some sort of signal to the men who had arrived with him, for they arrested Jesus straight away and took him to the high priest to stand trial.

All the disciples ran away and disappeared at this point, except Peter and me. We followed, but only at a distance, mind you. Fortunately, I know the high priest and so was able to get in to his courtyard where Jesus had been taken. After a minute, I realized that Peter was still waiting outside. I'd forgotten that he does not know the high priest, so I went back and brought Peter in with me. And we watched.

How do you shape up when you're asked to do something?
John and the others . . . well, they fell asleep.

When God asks something of you, do you have a 'sleep equivalent'?
Maybe you get distracted, or busy, or just plain don't want to do it.

Let's look at Luke 10:38–42:
Jesus and his disciples were visiting Mary and Martha. The Bible says that Martha 'opened her home to him' (verse 38).

What about your home?
Is Jesus welcome?

And what about your life?
Is Jesus welcome in your life?
Is he welcome in you?
Are there some bits you try to hide, or do you open up every part to him?
Welcome him in to every 'room'?

So, Jesus arrived and was welcomed.
But then it seems that Martha was so busy trying to see
that everything was ready,
so distracted by her preparations,
that she forgot to make time for Jesus.

Do you do that?
Forget to make time for him?

Martha's sister, Mary, on the other hand, sat with Jesus
and listened to him.
Which made Martha mad.
There was Martha, rushing around, trying to get
everything just right for their guest, and Mary was not
even helping her out!
So Martha complained to Jesus.

Isn't that interesting?
The only time Martha spends with Jesus is when she
wants to complain.
When she wants to have a moan.

Can the same be said of you?
Is complaining, crisis time the only time you spend with
Jesus?

And Martha is moaning because Mary is close to Jesus.
Is leaving things undone.
Is sitting at Jesus' feet.

Jesus says to Martha, 'Mary has chosen what is better' (verse 42).

Mary has chosen what is better . . .

But let's not forget that 'better' was an option for Martha, too.
She just didn't choose it.
In choosing not to leave things undone,
Martha chose not to spend time with Jesus.

Did it really matter if the house was not perfect?
If there was washing-up needing to be done, or if the cushions weren't straight?

Or what about all the things you busy yourself with?
Some matter, of course, but maybe some don't matter so much.
Are they really worth choosing not to spend time with Jesus for?

Psalm 16:11:
'You will fill me with joy in your presence.'

Mary would have known joy, Martha wouldn't.
And what was the key difference?
Presence.
Mary spent time in Jesus' presence.
And it filled her with joy.

Joy and presence go hand in hand – if you want joy,
spend time in God's presence.

And how about encouraging others to do the same?
Peter couldn't get into the courtyard because he didn't
know the high priest.
But John did.
And so John helped Peter to get in.

Some people can't enter into God's joy –
Maybe because they don't know God.
Maybe because they don't know how to get to him.
But you do.

So, will you help them into God's presence?
Will you show them the way?
And help them find joy?

Lord God,

I can be like Martha.
Always busy.
Forgetting to stop and take time with you.
I find it hard to leave things – help me to know when and what I should leave undone.
Lord, I sometimes get jealous of Marys.
They seem so content and resting in you.
Always choosing 'something better' when I don't seem to be able to.
Please help that to change.
I want to choose something better, too.
So, here and now, I choose to find joy in your presence.
And to show it to others.
Every day.

Amen

John's Jottings

Show
joy

My response:

Day 23

Jesus' trial was awful. Really awful. I could hardly look but at the same time, I couldn't look away. Soldiers beat Jesus up, totally humiliated him . . . and then the sentence came: Crucifixion. The absolute worst sentence possible.

I went to the cross where he was nailed. People were shouting at him and mocking him. Laughing at him. Only a handful of us were truly upset. Mary was there. I can't imagine what it must have been like to see your son being crucified. I mean, Jesus is my best friend, but he is her son. And he hasn't even done anything wrong.

Then, while he was hanging there, Jesus looked at me. I will never forget that look as he asked me to look after Mary. He was basically asking me to be a son to her, the son that he could no longer be. I had a lump in my throat. What an honour to be chosen, though. After Jesus had died, I took Mary home with me. We still can't believe that Jesus has gone; the whole thing is like a bad dream that we can't wake up from.

In the midst of his anguish on the cross, Jesus manages to speak.

He gasps out to John, 'Look after my mum.'

Jesus was thinking of others.

Crucifixion was one of the most horrible, painful ways to die.

Not only that, it was humiliating, as people came to watch and ridicule.

And yet, Jesus thought of others.

Sometimes it can be hard to think of others.

Life is busy, there is lots going on, our time is taken up with our own business and our own struggles, without trying to fit other people in.

Or maybe we sometimes just plain don't want to bother with other people.

They are annoying, time-consuming, interrupting, difficult . . .

Philippians 2:4 (NASB):

'Do not merely look out for your own personal interests, but also for the interests of others.'

What does it mean to look out for the interests of others?

Well, it means to look for the best for them.

To try to see where they are coming from.

To want things to go well for them and to do what you can to make that happen.

That's what Jesus did – he knew that Mary was having a difficult time and so he looked at the situation from her point of view.

And her point of view was that she had lost a son,
she was grieving
and she was alone.

So Jesus gave her a son.
Someone to share her grief
and someone to keep her company.

Jesus met her need.
Just as he can meet your need.

Who did Jesus choose when he wanted someone to
look after his mother?
Wanted someone to do a job for him?
He chose the one who stayed at the cross.

The other disciples had fled.
They had run away.
But John stayed at the cross.
And Jesus entrusted Mary to him.
What a privilege for John!

Sometimes, Jesus asks us to stay at the cross.
To go through the tough times.
To allow him to prepare us.

Watching her son die must have been one of the
hardest things Mary had ever had to do.
And Jesus gave her John.
John, who had been through the hardest time with her.

John, who had been right there.
If, later, Mary needed to talk about it, he knew.
If she didn't want to talk about it, he knew.
And he only knew because he had stayed at the cross.
Jesus chose him because he had stayed at the cross.

It can be easy to gloss over the crucifixion.
We don't like to think about it too much.
Maybe it is easier to join the disciples who ran away.

Do you spend time at the cross?
Spend time sharing in Jesus' sufferings?
Sharing what's on his heart?
Letting him prepare you?

Romans 8:17:

*'We are [God's] children [and] heirs . . . if indeed
we share in his sufferings in order that we may
also share in his glory.'*

Lord God,

The cross is hard.
Thank you that you did it.
That you hung there – for me.
Lord, staying at the cross is hard.
But I will do it if that's what you want.
Or I will try.
Help me to have the courage to go through the
tough times because, only then,
can I truly share in your glory.

Amen

John's Jottings

Don't run
away

My response:

Day 24

One of Jesus' disciples went and asked for Jesus' body. Joseph of Arimathea has always been quite a secret follower of Jesus, but he is not so secret any more, it seems. He wanted to honour Jesus by burying him in his own new tomb. But, unbelievably, the Pharisees are still concerned about Jesus.

This time, they seem to think that someone might steal the body and claim that Jesus is alive. Joseph had already placed a large stone across the front of the tomb but that wasn't enough for the Pharisees – they posted a guard as well! I know Jesus mentioned things that suggested he might be raised to life but, even so, all this guard business seems a bit over the top to me.

To be honest, I feel a bit in limbo – I can't get used to Jesus being gone. I miss him. And then there is Mary. Of course I am glad that Jesus asked me to look after her, as is she (I think). But at the end of the day, I'm not Jesus.

Jesus' body is taken down and put in a tomb, with instructions that it be guarded in order to stop people getting to him.
Let's personalize this with a question – what 'guards' do you have in your life? Guards that stop you getting to Jesus?

Or that stop you coming to him properly,
stop you having an open relationship with him?
Maybe fear.
Maybe guilt.
Maybe busy-ness.
Maybe selfishness.
Maybe apathy.
Maybe resentment.
Maybe a feeling of being unworthy.
Maybe . . . ?

Or maybe guards that other people put there:
Ridicule.
Demands.
Lack of understanding.
. . . ?

Jesus said, Revelation 3:20:
'Here I am! I stand at the door and knock. If anyone
hears my voice and opens the door, I will come in'.

Let's pick up a few things from this verse:
'Here I am!'
Jesus is not going anywhere.
Wherever you go and whatever you go through,
Jesus says, 'Hi! I'm here, too.'

'I stand at the door and knock.'
Whatever doors/guards you have, Jesus is not put off by
them.

He still stands there.
There's nothing that can scare him away.

'If anyone hears my voice . . .'
He's speaking – are you listening?

'. . . and opens the door . . .'
It's up to you.
He can deal with your doors, with your guards,
but you need to open them to him.

'. . . I will come in'.
When you do open your life up to God, he will
come in.

And you will find everything you need.

Paul wrote, in Philippians 4:19:
'And my God will meet all your needs according to his
glorious riches in Christ Jesus.'

All. Your. Needs.

Let's look at a parable Jesus told, Luke 15:11–32:
A man is fed up.
He is dissatisfied with his life.
His life consists of working with his father in a good
business and enjoying all the benefits that this provides.
And yet he is still fed up.

So he decides that he would really be better off taking matters into his own hands.
Going off and doing his own thing – that will make him much happier than helping his father.

So off he goes.
And he finds lots of substitutes for his father:
Parties, money, friends, popularity.
He knew that he could meet his own needs!

These substitutes keep him going for a while, but he can't sustain them.
Invitations stop, money dwindles, friends walk out.
Life has never been this hard before.

And then, finally, the man realizes the key difference – his father.
His own efforts are nothing compared to what his father can give him!
What's the point in struggling when there is no need?
And so the man heads home . . .

Do you struggle when there is no need?
When you have a God who is just waiting for you to turn to him?
To let him in?
To let him meet your needs?

Why not stop struggling and open that door?

Lord God,

Thank you that you are there.
Even when I refuse to open the door, you don't go anywhere.
But I don't know why I refuse, Lord –
I know that life is so much better when I share it with you.
Help me not to try to find 'God-substitutes'.
They don't exist anyway.
You are the best and I can't improve on the best!
Please come in.

Amen

John's Jottings

God meets
my needs

My response:

Day 25

I've seen another Mary today – Mary Magdalene. She came to get me because she could hardly believe what she'd seen: She had been to Jesus' tomb really early this morning. She wanted to look at it and to anoint Jesus' body with spices. Maybe she had forgotten about the big stone in front of the tomb, I don't know. But anyway, it didn't matter because when she got there, the stone had already been moved! She couldn't believe it. She came straight to tell Peter and me, and the two of us ran to the tomb to see for ourselves. I'm a faster runner than Peter, so I got there first and looked inside. I saw that Mary was right. Jesus was not there!

Peter and I went home – we wanted to tell other people about what we'd seen. But Mary stayed outside the tomb. Apparently, she was standing there crying when suddenly, through her tears, she saw Jesus! But she didn't recognize him; she thought he was the gardener. He asked her why she was crying so she asked him if he knew where the body had been taken to. And he replied with one word: 'Mary.' And then Mary knew. She knew it was Jesus. Jesus was alive! Jesus is alive!

So now another Mary enters the story. Let's think about her.

The Bible tells us that Mary had not forgotten about the stone at all.
Imagine her, getting up early, gathering spices, setting off for the tomb.
Worrying throughout about how she would move the stone from the entrance of the tomb when she got there, but going anyway.
And, when she got there, the stone had been moved!
So she had spent her time worrying unnecessarily, concerned about a problem that didn't even exist . . .
Are you like Mary?
Spending time chewing over worries and problems that 'might happen'?
The 'what ifs?'

There is a saying:
'Do not worry about tomorrow, God is already there.'
Grab hold of the truth of this; cling on tight and don't let it go.
Whatever happens or doesn't happen, God is there.

So, despite not having an answer to her 'how', Mary set off.
And the how became clear.
Sometimes we need to follow God without having all the answers.
He gives us enough light for the next step – but not necessarily the whole staircase.

Isaiah 42:16:

'"I will lead the blind by ways they have not known, along unfamiliar paths I will guide them; I will turn the darkness into light before them and make the rough places smooth. These are the things I will do; I will not forsake them."'

Mary saw Jesus *through her tears.*
Mary was upset.
She was bewildered.
She was crying . . . and yet she saw Jesus.

What do you see through your tears?
When you are upset, bewildered, crying – what do you see?
Do you look through your problems,
your worries, your confusion
and see Jesus?

Because Jesus is there.
Waiting for you to look.
Waiting for you to see him.
He is with you in your tears.

And, one day, your tears will be wiped away.
They really will.

Revelation 21:4:

'"[God] will wipe every tear from [your] eyes . . . There will be no more . . . crying or pain."'

No. More. Pain.

Jesus *spoke her name* – 'Mary.'
Just one word.
And one word was enough.
Mary knew.
She knew who he was.
But how did she know?

Because she recognized Jesus' voice.
And how did she recognize his voice?
Because she'd heard him say her name before.

Mary had spent time with Jesus.
She'd heard him.
She'd listened to him.
And so she recognized his voice.

Even though she was having a tough time,
she recognized his voice.
Even though she was feeling overwhelmed,
she recognized his voice.
Even though it seemed unlikely,
she recognized his voice.

Do you recognize Jesus' voice?
Do you listen for it?

He speaks – will you take time to recognize and listen to
him?

Despite everything, will you let him speak?

Let him speak your name.

Isaiah 43:1 (NLT):
*'"Do not be afraid, for I have ransomed you.
I have called you by name; you are mine."'*

Lord God,

My worries can be big.
Like the stone.
Really big.
And often unnecessary.
But I just get stuck in them.
Help me to see you through my tears, fears and confusion.
Help me to look.
Help me to listen.
Help me to recognize you and to let you speak.
To let you share my pain, my tears, my struggles.
To hear you speak my name.

Amen

John's Jottings

Jesus calls
my name

My response:

Day 26

I came across my diary this morning. I have neglected it for years. Decades, even. Reading back, what happened back then seems a lifetime ago. After Jesus came back to life, we spent time with him – chatting, picnics on the beach, enjoying his company, receiving instructions from him. Then one day he was taken up into heaven. We actually saw him go! Since then, we have been trying to do what he told us to do – tell other people about him.

And people are believing in him. Really believing, and wanting to follow his teachings. The group is growing. Writing seems to have grown on me, too, and I have written to the new Christians. There are other teachings going around, things like 'Jesus was not really God'?! So I want to encourage the new believers not to get taken in. I want them to be sure of what they believe.

It's easy to get taken in, isn't it?

Let's look at Exodus 32:
Moses has disappeared up a mountain to talk to God, and the rest of the Israelites are waiting for him to come back.

And waiting.
And waiting.
But Moses does not come back.
Eventually, someone suggests that maybe it would be a good idea to take matters into their own hands.
They don't know what's happened to Moses.
Best just to make a god of their own.
And the idea takes on, and on, and on
until, at last, the whole community is saying OK.
Even though God has done so much for them, has brought them out of slavery, has protected them . . .
they are saying OK.
They've been led astray but they are saying OK.
Because it seems like a good idea to them.

When God first helped them miraculously escape from Egypt, they would probably never have imagined turning away from him.
And yet now they are.
So God sends Moses back down the mountain.
Moses goes, and finds the people worshipping a golden calf that they've made.
And Moses is carrying tablets of stone which God has written on:
'You shall have no other gods before me' (Exodus 20:3).

When we get taken in, when we stop letting God be number one, we disobey this commandment.
And not just taken in by things other people say or do.
What about worry?

Or work?
Or friends?
Or partner?
Or plans?
Or ourselves?

Do they become more important than God?
Become 'gods' in their own right?

'You shall have no other gods before me.'

John didn't want the new believers to get taken in, to get led astray, to stop having God as number one.
And so what did he advise?

1 John 2:24:
'See that what you have heard from the begin-ning remains in you. If it does, you also will remain in the Son and in the Father.'

Know what you believe.
Know your God.
And stick with that knowledge.
Don't let it go.

But it is also easy to think that getting taken in, being led astray, is something that only happens to other people.
You feel strong, sure of your faith, know what's what . . .

Let's just note some wise words from the apostle Paul:

1 Corinthians 10:12:
'So, if you think you are standing firm, be careful that you don't fall!'

Be careful, it is possible to think that you are safe from falling.
Be aware.

1 Peter 5:8–10:
'Be self-controlled and alert . . . And the God of all grace, who called you to his eternal glory in Christ, after you have suffered a little while, will himself restore you and make you strong, firm and steadfast.'

Don't get taken in by anything or anyone other than God.

As John wrote (1 John 5:21 NLT):
'Dear children, keep away from anything that might take God's place in your hearts.'

Lord God,

Thank you that you are there and that you are faithful.
I'm sorry for the times I get distracted and think that going astray from you is OK.
Or, even if I don't actually think it's OK, I still do it. I lose my focus.
Help me to be careful not to lose touch with you.
Thank you that you have promised to restore me. And that you will do it.
Help me to stay alert so that I don't let anything take your place.

Amen

John's Jottings

Let God be
number one

My response:

Day 27

Well, I've just written another letter because I am a bit worried. People are still being taken in by false teaching. These false teachers are clever; they make things sound so reasonable – but they are not speaking the truth. And truth is so important. I long for the church to follow the truth. So I wrote to advise them that it might be best not to spend time with false teachers. And I encouraged the church to continue to love each other; I remember Jesus was very clear about the importance of that.

So, the church still seems to be being taken in by false teachings.
There is not a one-off cure, we need to be alert at all times.
As we saw yesterday, 1 Corinthians 10:12:
'If you think you are standing firm, be careful that you don't fall!'
Never stop being careful . . .

Truth is so important.
Pilate, at Jesus' trial, asked, 'What is truth?' (John 18:38).
Jesus himself had already answered that question when he said,

'I am the way and the truth and the life' (John 14:6).

Next time you are unsure about whether something is true or false,
right or wrong, yes or no . . .
See how that thing or situation measures up before Jesus.
Is it something he'd be happy with?

We need to be people who speak the truth, speak Jesus, into situations around us.

But sometimes it's hard.
There seem to be so many 'truths' around, so many people convinced of what they believe.
So many people ready to take offence.

Ephesians 4:15:

'Speaking the truth in love, we will in all things grow up into him who is the Head, that is, Christ.'

This is the key – love.
Speaking the truth can be hard, as can hearing it.
But if we love each other enough, and want to grow together, we'll do it.
We won't want anyone to be going astray.

Let's look at Jethro, in Exodus 18:
Jethro's son-in-law, Moses, has been given a pretty important job by God.

Moses is leading the Israelites, God's chosen people, into a new land.

One day, Jethro decides to go to visit Moses.
When he arrives at the camp, Moses comes out to meet him and they head into Moses' tent to have a good catch-up.
Moses excitedly tells Jethro about all that has happened recently:
God has helped the Israelites escape slavery in Egypt!
Moses went and spoke to Pharaoh!
God used Moses to prove to Pharaoh that God is not a God to be ignored!
The two men probably talk well into the night.

The next day, Jethro wakes up.
When he comes out of his tent, Moses is nowhere to be found.
So Jethro goes to look for Moses and finds him listening to the people.
Or, to be specific, listening to the people's problems and concerns.
One by one, people are coming to Moses to ask his advice.

Jethro leaves them to it and goes for a walk around the camp.
After a couple of hours, he goes back, figuring that Moses will have finished now.
But no.

There is still a queue of people waiting to see Moses.
So Jethro goes off again.
And comes back a couple of hours later.
And then again at lunchtime.
Then an hour after that.
And an hour after that.
But Moses still hasn't finished.

Eventually, but not until the evening, the queue is gone
and Jethro is able to speak to Moses. But what to say?
Jethro has seen that Moses is doing too much and is
going to wear himself out.
But Jethro is also aware that Moses probably won't want
to hear that!
And Moses is Moses. The man chosen by God.

Jethro looks at Moses.
Tired from the day, exhausted by trying to do the right
thing, his son-in-law . . . and Jethro remembers how
much he loves Moses.
He loves him too much not to tell him the truth.
So Jethro speaks up:

'Moses, you are doing too much.'
Which, in the end, leads Moses to get some people to
share the job with him.
Which makes life better for Moses.

Moses is not the only one to know what it is like to be
tired and worn out.

There are people like that all around us.
Tired, hurting, confused . . . churches are full of them.
Do you notice?
And, if you do, do you look at them with love?
And, if you do, do you love them enough to tell them
the truth?
The truth about God and how to follow his ways, even
when it is hard?

And what about yourself?
Do you love yourself enough to tell yourself the truth?
To take an honest look inside and acknowledge where
perhaps your life and priorities are not what God would
want?

Loving can be hard.
But not as hard as not loving at all.

Ephesians 4 goes on to say (verse 16):
'From him [Christ] the whole body, joined and held
together by every supporting ligament, grows and
builds itself up in love, as each part does its work.'

Are you doing your part, in love, to help his body to
grow?

Jesus said, 'Love each other as I have loved you' (John
15:12).
Actually, he commanded it.

Part of Jesus' love was that he never, ever turned people away from the truth.
He never led them astray, either by speaking or not speaking out.
Or by the way he lived his life.

John 13:35:

'"By this all men will know that you are my disciples, if you love one another."'

Lord God,

The truth can be hard.
Hard to hear and hard to tell.
Help me to be faithful and loving when I need to speak the truth to people.
And help me to be gracious when they need to speak the truth to me.
May your church be known as your disciples because of the love we have for one another.

Amen

John's Jottings

Love
truth

My response:

Day 28

I wrote to my friend, Gaius, today. Just a short note as I am hoping to meet with him soon. I am old now so don't know how many more opportunities I will have. I just wanted to write and say 'well done' to him, he is really holding on to God's truth. And he is welcoming people and showing hospitality to visitors.

On the other hand, Diotrephes, a member of the church, refuses to show hospitality to the people that I am sending to help them. And, even worse, he throws people out of the church if they welcome them! Plus he gossips about us.

I am so thankful for Gaius and his faith in God.

John is writing this letter to encourage Gaius.
To assure Gaius that he is doing a good job.
Basically, to say, 'Well done!'

It's a good thing to do.
When was the last time you said 'well done' to someone?
Told them that you are thankful for them?
Told them they were doing a good job?
We are called to be encouragers!

1 Thessalonians 5:11:

'Encourage one another and build each other up.'

Gaius was standing firm and sticking with God,
despite opposition from people such as Diotrephes.

Let's look at Noah, starting at Genesis 6:
Noah lives in pretty tough times.
Wicked people are everywhere, no one cares about God.
In fact, God's heart is filled with pain and he is sorry that
he even bothered to make people in the first place.
Except for Noah, that is.

The Bible tells us that Noah was a righteous man who
walked with God.
Noah was obviously managing to stick to his beliefs
despite what was going on around him.
One day, God says to Noah, 'OK. Enough's enough. I am
going to end all this wickedness and violence.
I am going to destroy the earth.
But not you. So build a big boat.
I am going to send so much rain that nothing outside of
that boat will survive.'

Right!
Noah could have said, 'People will think I'm crazy and
they already think I'm odd.'
He could have said, 'How am I supposed to build a boat
that size?'
He could have said, 'What's rain?' (See Genesis 2:5.)

But he didn't.
What Noah did say was 'OK.'
And he got to work.

Day after day, Noah hammers away.
And day after day, people probably think he has gone mad.
But nevertheless, Noah hammers away.
And the boat is built.

Noah takes animals on board.
He takes his wife on board.
He takes his family on board.
He maybe makes a futile attempt to persuade other people to get on board.
Finally, he climbs on board himself.

And the rains come.

Flick forward through the Bible to Hebrews chapter 11, and what do we find?
Noah, being commended for what he did.
In fact, we find a whole list of people being commended.
A whole list of people getting a 'well done' from God!
Well done for obeying God.
Well done for standing firm.

What about you?
Does God commend you?

As you look back on each day, have you given God opportunities to say 'well done'?

One 'well done' opportunity we can pick up from John's diary entry today concerns gossip.
Gossip can be so easy to fall into, can't it?
Spreading or listening to rumours about other people.
Passing on other people's secrets just for the thrill of being the one with some news.
But it is not helpful.
To you or anyone else.
Be careful to get the balance between 'speaking the truth in love' (Ephesians 4:15) and merely gossiping.
The former wants the best for all concerned.
The latter wants the best for the gossiper.
And it's the former that will get the 'well done'.

Matthew 25:23 (NLT):
'"Well done, my good and faithful servant . . . Let's celebrate together!"'

When you do give God these 'well done' opportunities, and you will if you live to please him, don't forget to share them with him.
To enjoy them with him.
To celebrate with him.
To share in his happiness (Matthew 25:23).

Because when God can say 'well done' to you, you make him smile – really smile!

Day 28

Lord God,

Thank you that when you ask me to do something,
you don't ask me to do it alone.
You are there with me, every step of the way.
Encouraging me.
Cheering me on.
Waiting to say 'well done'.
I want to give us something to celebrate.
I want to give you lots of opportunities to say 'well
done' to me.
I want to make you really smile.
I love you, Lord.

Amen

John's Jottings

Make God
smile

My response:

Day 29

Well, change of venue for me. I have been exiled, for my faith and for telling other people about Jesus, and am now on the island of Patmos. The Romans are making things really hard for all Christians, not just me. They want everyone to worship the emperor and are persecuting, even killing, people who refuse. It's really hard and some Christians are beginning to suggest compromise with the Romans. I have written to the churches to encourage them to remember that God is still in control and to remind them to trust him.

Times were hard, no question about it.
People were being killed for their faith.
It was tough – and so they wanted to compromise.

What about you when life gets tough?
You don't want to make it any harder.
You want to keep the status quo.
Do you compromise your relationship with God?
Say, 'I can follow God and other things at the same time?'

During John's exile, Jesus spoke to him.
And told him what to write to each of seven churches.

Let's look at what John wrote to the church at Laodicea
(Revelation 3):
'I know your deeds, that you are neither cold nor hot. I
wish you were either one or the other!' (verse 15).

'I know your deeds . . .'
Whatever you do, God knows.
Whatever you don't do, God knows.
Every opportunity to serve him you take or pass by, God
knows.

Psalm 139:1 (NLT):
'O Lord, you have examined my heart
and know everything about me.'

'. . . you are neither cold nor hot.'
Basically, this seems to be saying that they don't care
whether they follow God or not.
They don't feel strongly either way.
For God or against him, they really don't mind.

What about you?
Do you care whether you are truly following God?
Is your spiritual life just drifting along?

'I wish you were one or the other!'
Make up your mind.

Be certain.
Don't just drift along.
Lukewarm.
Keeping the status quo.
Not exactly on fire.

Let's look at Cain, in Genesis 4:
Cain is a farmer. He grows crops.
One day, he decides to give some of his crops to God as an offering.

But Cain seems to be a bit lukewarm, a bit neither hot nor cold about it.
He wants to offer something to God but, at the same time, he doesn't want to give his best crops.
He wants them for himself.
And so he doesn't offer them.
He compromises instead, and just gives some crops.

And so God is not pleased – because God knows.
He knows exactly what Cain has and hasn't done.

Then Cain realizes that God *is* pleased with his brother, Abel, who has offered God his very best.
Which makes Cain angry.

God wants to know why he's angry:
'Come on, Cain.
I would have been pleased with you, too, if you had given to me wholeheartedly.

With the right attitude.
But you didn't.
You compromised.
You didn't want to lose out,
so you compromised.'

And that compromise led Cain, fuelled by jealousy, to murder his brother.
Which God knew about.
Despite Cain trying to hide it.
Because God knows our deeds.
That compromise also led to Cain going away.
So Cain went out from God's presence (verse 16).

Cain's compromise didn't work.
And he ended up far away from God.
That's what happens when we compromise between God and other things.
Eventually, we find ourselves out of God's presence.
Out of enjoying a relationship with him.
Out of options.
Because compromise doesn't work.

Matthew 6:24:
'"No-one can serve two masters. Either he will hate the one and love the other, or he will be devoted to the one and despise the other. You cannot serve both God and Money."'

And it's not just money.
It is anything that becomes more of a boss, has more control over you, than God.

So don't compromise.

Lord God,

Lukewarm is not a good word!
Can it be applied to me, spiritually?
Help me to answer this question honestly.
Am I compromising?
Trying to have two bosses?
Lord, I want you to be the only boss in my life.
And I know you want the job!
You are the best candidate, hands down –
so help me to stop compromising
and to let you get on with it.

Amen

John's Jottings

Don't compromise

My response:

Day 30

After years in exile on Patmos, I have been released. The revelations God gave me there were amazing, confusing, encouraging, disturbing . . . and lots more. But the overriding thing is that Jesus is coming again. He really is!

Flicking back through my diary, so much has happened – healings, blessings, tough times, happy times. But Jesus is the common theme in every diary entry. He runs through every page, and that is just how it should be. He has changed me so much – did I mention that I used to have such a temper? (Remember that time I wanted to call down fire in Samaria!) But that was the old me; Jesus gave me a new start.

My life on earth is nearly over. I started writing this diary because I was curious about Jesus. I don't need to be curious any more, because I know him. And I am going to keep getting to know him. There will be no more diary entries here. I will be starting a new chapter in heaven. An eternal chapter – with Jesus.

Imagine you are a tree.
When trees are chopped down, inside the trunk is a circle for every year that the tree has been growing.

In a sense, these circles mark the life of that tree.
They literally run right through it.

If John's diary were a tree, Jesus would be running
through every circle.
Jesus is the inspiration behind every page.

John is now nearing the end of his earthly life.
He is about to be 'chopped down'.
And, ever since he met Jesus, Jesus will be in every
circle.

What about you?
Would Jesus be running through the years and circles of
your life?
Or would some be filled with other things?
Would he influence all of your diary entries, or would he
be a hasty afterthought?
An 'also happened to be there'?
A PS?

Let's change the question slightly:
Will he be running through your life from now on?
We can't change the past.
John couldn't change the fact that he'd been
hot-tempered.
But by sticking with Jesus, John was able to write about
loving each other.
Not lashing out.

Jesus is able to change things for the better – that's why John kept close to him!

Jesus said, when talking about Jerusalem:

Luke 13:34 (NLT):
'"How often I have wanted to gather your children together as a hen protects her chicks beneath her wings, but you wouldn't let me."'

I'm here.
You don't have to do it on your own.
I want to help . . . but you're not letting me.

John let Jesus help, and his life was changed.
Will you let Jesus change your life for the better?

At the start of his diary, John was curious about Jesus.
At the end, he knows Jesus.
At the start, he couldn't figure out how it was possible for anyone to be greater than John the Baptist.
At the end, having spent time with Jesus, he knows that there is no comparison.
And he testifies to that in his final letter.

Revelation 5:12:
'"Worthy is the Lamb, who was slain, to receive power and wealth and wisdom and strength and honour and glory and praise!"'

Praise his name.
Always.
He is worthy!

Lord God,

Thank you that you change my life for the better.
Help me to come to you and let you do it.
You are the only one who really can.
The only one that is worthy of my praise.
Help me never to make you a PS –
You are worthy of more!
So much more.
Thank you for all you have done for me.
I look forward to what you will do . . . and
I am going to stick close to you because I don't
want to miss it!
Amen

John's Jottings

Jesus is
worthy!

My response:

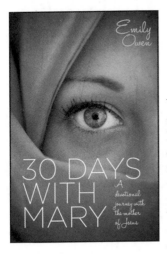

30 Days with Mary
A devotional journey with the mother of Jesus
Emily Owen

What must it have been like to be Mary, the mother of the Son of God?

In *30 Days with Mary* we look at her diary, sharing in her trials and challenges, fears and joys, from her teenage encounter with an angel, to the awesomeness of realizing her crucified son is alive again. The diary excerpts lead us in contemplation, challenging our own relationship with Christ and, in so doing, draw us closer to him.

978-1-86024-935-8

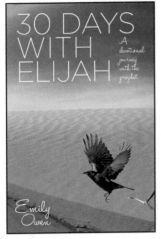

30 Days with Elijah
A devotional journey with the prophet
Emily Owen

If Elijah had written a diary, what would it be like?

Here is a chance to find out, from his experiences with the prophets of Baal, to running from Jezebel, and meeting with God! With thirty days of 'diary extracts', followed by contemplative and thought-provoking teaching, this is a gentle yet challenging book. There are useful questions, and prayers to encourage us to 'be an Elijah'!

978-1-86024-937-2

Printed in Great Britain
by Amazon